LAND OF THE FIREWEED

A Young Woman's Story of
Alaska Highway Construction Days

By Hope Morritt

Alaska Northwest Publishing Company

130 Second Avenue South, Edmonds, Washington 98020
(206) 774-4111

Library of Congress Cataloging-in-Publication Data

Morritt, Hope.
    Land of the fireweed.

1. Morritt, Hope.   2. Northwest, Canadian — Biography.
3. Alaska Highway.   I. Title.
F1060.9.M875A34   1986   971.9   85-15709
ISBN 0-88240-307-9

Photographs by Hope Morritt and Dan Cameron, except as noted
Cover photograph by Sharon Paul
Maps by Laura J. DeAnna

Alaska Northwest Publishing Company
130 Second Ave. S., Edmonds, WA 98020

Printed in U.S.A.

I dedicate this book to my son, Ian Michael Cameron, and my daughter, Lynn Marie Cameron. Without their constant urging and support, I doubt I would have put pen to paper to record these memories.

Land of the Fireweed, *I return once more*
to feel the call of yesterdays in bone
and blood, moccasins dancing on the shore
of love and lust; epitaphs in stone
marking each step along a distant road
forged by the stench of war and sweat of men.
I want to see again that mother lode
of savage primrose scaling fen to fen
the wounded land, covering blackened scourge
of forest fires that rape and plunder earth
prodding the wind to sing a haunting dirge
for that which might have been in hope, rebirth.

Magenta fireweed, fling your mantle high
to seal the wounds as I go riding by.

Hope Morritt

Acknowledgements . . .

I would like to thank the Canada Council for its assistance in preparing this book.

Also, I would like to thank Flora MacDonald for her untiring efforts in assisting me with research; Dan Cameron for the time he spent remembering pertinent facts; the historians at the Directorate of History, National Defence Headquarters, Ottawa, for their assistance in helping me dig up information on the Northwest Highway System; the Atlin Historical Society, Atlin, B.C.; Yukon Department of Heritage and Cultural Resources, Whitehorse, Y.T.; General Geof. Walsh; Brig. J.R.B. Jones; Georgina Murray Keddell; Jim Quong; and the many people who were "there," and who phoned or wrote of their memories.

I have also used my own scrapbooks, notes, pictures, letters and memorabilia to launch this book.

—Hope Morritt

MAPS

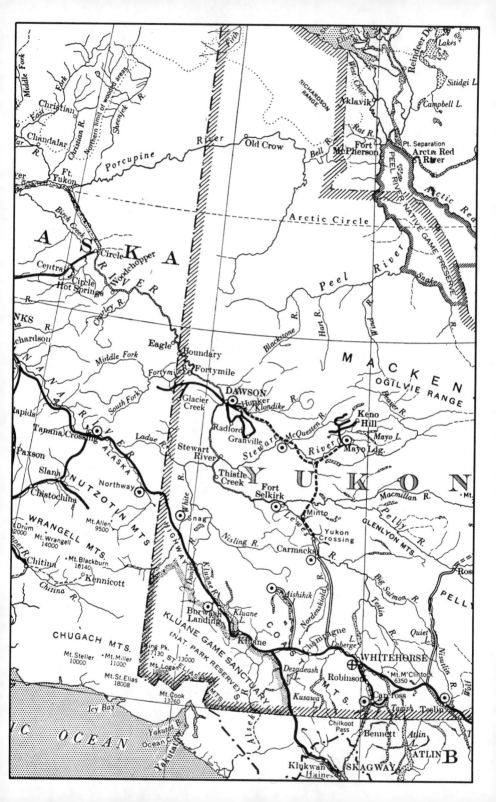

Chapter 1

A remote mountain valley where the hulks of wartime bombers are rotting away. Fragmented pictures came at me . . . flying boxcars tumbling earthward, spiralling toward inevitable death.

I studied the handsome, dark-haired pilot who sat near my desk in the newsroom at the *Edmonton Bulletin* in Edmonton, Alberta. It was spring, 1945. The airman was dressed in the gray-blue uniform of the Royal Canadian Air Force. Pilot's wings were displayed proudly above his left breast pocket; a peaked cap, bashed out of shape from wearing aircraft headphones, sat jauntily on his head.

"You're not kidding? There really *is* a valley of lost planes?"

He searched through his tunic pockets, and after a few moments held up a wide bracelet of shiny metal.

"I have a friend in Whitehorse who's selling rings, bracelets . . . all kinds of jewelry pieces he makes from metal he's scrounged off sagging hulks of aircraft in The Valley. Here."

He handed me the bracelet . . . chunky pieces of shiny, silvery metal strung together with strong, elastic threads. I slid it on my arm.

"For me?"

"Sure, kid. I got one like it for my mother. I'll tell you . . . Brad, my friend . . . he's selling those things like cotton candy at a circus."

"And they're really made from metal off aircraft in The Valley?"

"You doubt me, kid? Look . . . Brad's honest. I flew him over The Valley for the first time over a year ago. Then, he rented a Junkers and flew in on his own."

"*Flew* in?"

"Sure. He's a pilot. Flew Spits during the war."

"Do these . . . these lost aircraft belong to . . . to anybody in particular?"

"You bet. Once upon a time they belonged to Uncle Sam."

He lit a cigarette, inhaled, then slowly exhaled. "I've been curious about that valley for over a year, ever since I first came

1

to the Northwest on posting . . . ever since I heard American pilots talking about Million Dollar Valley."

"Million Dollar Valley?"

"Yeah . . . a million dollar's worth of aircraft are locked in there."

He settled back in his chair, and with the air of a veteran storyteller, related a spine-tingling tale of war bombers (Marauders) that lost their way while en route to Alaska in December, 1941.

After the Japanese attack on Pearl Harbor, the U.S. War Department decided to send aerial reinforcements to Alaska to fortify that area in case of attack. The logical route for the bombers to follow was the string of airfields in northern Canada developed by the bush pilots of the 1930s. These airfields were strung out like beads on a necklace, situated at Grande Prairie, Alberta; Fort St. John and Fort Nelson, British Columbia; Watson Lake and Whitehorse, Yukon Territory. The Canadian government had just installed radio ranges along this necklace to the Alaska border, and work was continuing to update the fields.

On December 10, 1941, thirteen B-26 bombers left Boise, Idaho, for Fairbanks, Alaska. The young pilots were not used to flying in a rugged wilderness like the mountainous territory in the Far North. The crews were not even wearing winter clothing, nor were they equipped with winter gear or rations for survival in the bush.

These bombers were to play "follow the leader," which was probably a good arrangement, except that somewhere along the way five aircraft lost their leader.

By January 25, eight had arrived at Ladd Field in Alaska, two never did show up and it was presumed that they crashed "somewhere," and three made belly landings in the remote valley.

"And the crews?" I asked breathlessly, when Tim finished his tale.

"I heard they were air-lifted out by a bush pilot, quite a feat because that valley is ridged with fanglike peaks. I understand that later the U.S. Army Engineers building the Alaska Highway sent a detonator crew in to detonate the bombs."

"You mean those bombers were actually carrying bombs?"

"Apparently. Those guys were lucky, weren't they?"

"Wow. They sure were."

* * *

I'd met this airman, Tim Condon, in the spring of 1944 when I had taken a part-time job as a cub reporter with the *Edmonton*

Bulletin. He had been doing a little public relations work for the Royal Canadian Air Force, and I had been assigned to work with him on stories about the Far North. I had always found him exciting. Now, I slid a piece of paper into my typewriter.

"Look . . . let me get this down —" I stopped in mid-sentence when I saw him shake his head.

"Not this one, kid. This is my story. I don't want it headlined across the country."

"But —"

"No buts. I'm jealous of my valley. It's for me to write up some day."

I twisted the bracelet on my arm.

"What's the name of your friend, the one who's making jewelry?"

"Hey . . . there's a story for you. His name's Owen Bradley. He's got a small spread, a two-by-four place, in Whitehorse."

He stood, grinned, walked to the door of the newsroom, then turned and called back: "Would you believe there's an eerie pull, a strange gravity that keeps those bombers in the valley? Even if they *could* fly out, they'd never get airborne."

"What?" I shouted, incredulously.

He laughed impishly, and flung me a line from Robert Service: "There are strange things done in the midnight sun."

He saluted and was gone. A bold, cocksure man of twenty-five years, who in the last year had given me first-hand stories of a world I'd dreamed about since I had been a child. A world of adventure, ghostly valleys and people who did not fit into a mold. Owen Bradley and Tim Condon. I could not and would not forget them.

Chapter 2

The children born in Edmonton, Alberta, in the 1920s and 1930s were well aware of the land north of the 60th parallel and the pioneers who were pushing back this last frontier. In those days Edmonton was called "Gateway to the North." It was a kicking-off place for adventurers bound for the Yukon, Northwest Territories and Alaska. It was the place where bush pilots were heroes, where every kid followed excitedly the danger-riddled flights of Wop May, Punch Dickens, Grant McConachie and Leigh Brintnell. It didn't matter whether these pilots were hauling mail, fish or prospectors into and out of that big back-of-beyond . . . we hung on every word they spoke.

I grew up in the Norwood district of Edmonton, where several bush pilots had homes. Among them was Ralph Oakes, who later became a regular captain on Dakotas flying the Canadian Pacific run from Edmonton to Fairbanks. (These Dakotas were two-engine aircraft that carried twenty-eight passengers. They were called DC-3s in the United States, the "D" referring to Douglas Aircraft Co., which built them.) Bruce Wilson, who lived next door to my dad, was also a pilot. In 1945, Wilson was one of many airmen pioneering air freight services from Edmonton to the Northwest Territories, and prior to that, he had been a pilot training navigators at the Royal Canadian Air Force Air Observer School in Edmonton.

As children and teen-agers, my two sisters, friends and I often gathered at Wilson's home, where pilots would get together and talk of great moments in aviation history. My father, Herbert L. Morritt, joined us when he wasn't sorting mail in the downtown post office. Dad, too, had his stories to tell. He had seen Wiley Post take off in his white Lockheed monoplane in Edmonton in 1931. Post, the one-eyed aviator from Oklahoma, and his Australian navigator, Harold Gatty, were on a round-the-world flight. Their course had taken them from the United States to England, to Russia, across Siberia, over the Bering Sea to Alaska, and, on the home stretch, to Edmonton and New York.

4

The day before Post's arrival in Edmonton, dad said, a wild rainstorm pounded the city, turning the small airfield into a sea of mud. The monoplane (which Post had nicknamed "Winnie Mae") got down on the muddy runway, but a take-off was impossible. Jim Bell, manager of the airport, decided that the only solution was to get electricians to strip the overhead wires, including those of a trolley line, along the two-mile stretch of city street called Portage Avenue (later named Kingsway). Portage was one of the few paved streets in Edmonton at that time, dad said. With the wires temporarily removed, the "Winnie Mae" took off from pavement.

The Post landing and take-off put Edmonton in world news. My father said he was out on the sidewalk along Portage Avenue at dawn on July 1, 1931.

"It was very exciting, seeing this big white plane roar down the street, wingtips barely missing the light poles. Sometimes I thought my eyes were playing tricks on me. It seemed unreal . . . or perhaps surreal might be a better word . . . the cold, gray light of dawn, people hugging sidewalks, and this monstrous airplane straddling the streetcar tracks, its propeller spinning faster, faster until it lifted, made a wide arc and disappeared into the sun."

Dad always shook his head incredulously with the memory, then, stroking his chin thoughtfully, added, "Late that night I tuned in to my radio set and heard that Post and Gatty had landed at Roosevelt Field, New York. They had circled the globe in eight days, fifteen hours and fifty-one minutes, setting a record."

My father, who had a memory like a bear trap, often told us about a return trip by Post in 1935 when the pilot was accompanied by Will Rogers, the American humorist. Post landed in Edmonton on a sunny day in August en route to Siberia.

"He was able to use the airport runways for both landing and taking off on this second trip," dad informed us. "A crowd had gathered at the field to see him go, and I was there, too, as usual. This departure certainly wasn't as spectacular as the Portage Avenue one, but, in a way, it was memorable because Edmonton was the last civilized centre the two men saw. They crashed the next day near Point Barrow, Alaska, and both were killed."

My father had loved Will Rogers . . . his wit, easy manner . . . and I always noticed a sadness in his voice when he talked about this tragic end for a well-loved show biz personality.

The roar of airplanes overhead was often ear-shattering in our home in Edmonton, and dad threatened to take out special insurance on his house in case a monster missed the runway and landed on our roof. Teachers at Victoria High School, not far from the airport, complained of the noise. One day I was trying to listen to an algebra lecture by D.L. Shortliffe. "Shorty" paused while one of the sky demons roared overhead. When all was quiet, he grew red in the face and shouted, "Have you ever heard of anything more insane than building a hospital and a school in the backyard of an airport?"

* * *

Edmonton was in world news again in 1942, when thousands of United States troops poured into the city for the building of the Alaska Highway. The engineers for this priority job had decided that the highway route should follow the string of northern airfields set up by bush pilots in the 1930s.

On December 18, 1940, the Canadian government funded the building of aerodromes and the installation of radio ranges at these northern airfields. The ranges enabled pilots to navigate accurately without visual reference to the ground.

Shortly after the Japanese attack on Pearl Harbor, December 7, 1941, the U.S. government was seeking an airway to Alaska that would be relatively free from the danger of enemy attack. Canada's northern airfields — from Fort St. John to Whitehorse — were a logical choice.

In an article he wrote for a special edition of the *Edmonton Bulletin,* July 8, 1944, C.G. Power, Canada's minister of national defence for air, said, "Under war's compelling pressures, the scope of operations on these northern airfields went through a continuing process of expansion. While some of that expansion was due to Canadian needs, much of it was the result of American suggestion. The Canadian government, however, insisted that wherever permanent facilities or improvements are developed directly from a request of the United States, the cost will be borne by the Canadian government."

By the end of 1943, Canada had spent $46 million in development of these northern airfields and a further $6 million building emergency flight strips between the fields.

In 1940, incredible difficulties had to be surmounted in modernizing these northern airfields. Tons of supplies had to be moved hundreds of miles, through mountainous hinterland where roads did not exist. Seven months after work began, the airway from Edmonton to Whitehorse was usable by daylight. By the end of 1941, the radio beam was operating at all fields and flight strips from Edmonton to the Alaska border. By 1942, when troops and equipment were pouring into Canada from the United States to build the Alaska Highway, the U.S. Army Air Corps was flying bombers, fighters and transports along this route, using these airfields night and day, in good weather and bad. Canadian Pacific Airlines also was conducting regular, commercial flights along the route from Edmonton to Fairbanks.

In September, 1942, control of the fields became the responsibility of the RCAF's Northwest Air Command, with headquarters in Edmonton. The string of airports was known as the Northwest Staging Route.

* * *

My greatest desire in those days was to see that Far North I'd heard so much about next door at Bruce Wilson's. Meeting Tim Condon in the spring of 1944 and 1945 pushed me to put my dreams into action. There would be a quest for Hope Morritt — a quest for adventure, a quest to find aircraft that were rotting away in a valley more eerie than Headless Valley.

Old-timers in the Yukon speak with great awe of Headless Valley, where, according to legend, the gold streams are guarded by headless men. The valley, which follows the South Nahanni River in the southwest corner of the Northwest Territories, was first called Dead Man's Valley in 1905 to 1906 when the bodies of two brothers, Frank and Willie McLeod, were found without heads. The brothers had gone into the Nahanni country to look for gold, and, in the next half-century, the Valley guarded its gold well. Adventurers turned up as headless corpses, or they vanished without leaving a trace. Prospectors and trappers began to fear the Nahanni country, where high, rugged mountains were forbidding sentinels, and river canyons were so deep the walls obscured the sun.

By contrast, however, waterfalls in the valley were beautiful, the vegetation was thick and luxurious, and hot springs bubbled up from the earth's surface in winter and summer. But . . . Headless Valley did not have wartime bombers, like giant ghost ships, locked within its walls.

Once I had wanted to be a bush pilot and fly my own plane into remote regions of the North. I had not reckoned on the expense involved when I'd dreamed those idle dreams. Now, facing reality, I knew the next-best thing would be to get a job in the Yukon.

* * *

Valleys and gorges run deep in the Yukon Territory. One such valley cradled World War II bombers forced to crash-land in 1941.

In April of 1946, the U.S. Army presented to Canada exactly 1,221.4 miles of a gravelled, mountain road that was like a long, tangled ribbon threading its way through untamed hinterland.

I had followed with keen interest the building of that road in 1942. My father had declared the U.S. Army Engineers would not finish the road from Dawson Creek, British Columbia (Mile 0) to Fairbanks, Alaska (about 1,550 miles) in the allotted time of nine months. My sisters — Eileen and Pat — and I bet him that they would. In mid-March, 1942, Northern Alberta Railroad cars were bulging with U.S. troops and equipment bound for Dawson Creek. Nine months later, on November 21, two U.S. Army soldiers completed their drive over the full length of the pioneer road — Dawson Creek to Fairbanks — in two Army trucks.

"See," I told my dad, pointing out the item in the *Edmonton Journal.* "They made it."

He put his glasses on, and after studying the story at length, he looked at me, surprised delight spreading across his lean face. "Well . . . I'll be damned," he said.

* * *

Four years later, on November 22, 1946, a Friday, I walked into a personnel office in downtown Edmonton where the Canadian Army was hiring civilians to work at camps along the Alaska Highway. After giving me shorthand and typing tests, the young Army officer sat back in his swivel chair behind a desk and studied me.

"Are you going to school?" he asked.

"No," I replied indignantly, standing to the full measure of my five-foot, nine-inch height. "I've worked on and off for the last two years at the *Edmonton Bulletin,* in the newsroom, but wages were always poor. Two months ago I hired on with the Department of Veterans' Affairs —"

"Can you leave tomorrow?" he asked, interrupting.

"Tomorrow?" I echoed, surprised. "For what place?"

"Whitehorse."

My thoughts raced in confusion. I really hadn't thought that I would have a chance of landing a job when I had wandered into his office twenty minutes earlier. A friend of mine had been told by him the week before that there were no more jobs available in the Far North. Suddenly, the chance of a lifetime was within reach. I looked at my watch. It was noon. I could give the DVA my notice of termination this afternoon. My boss there wouldn't be happy with the short warning, but suddenly I didn't care.

"Yes. I can leave tomorrow," I blurted out.

"Good. Come back at five-thirty today for further instructions and your airplane ticket."

"One question?"

"Shoot."

"You said I'd be starting out at $135 a month. That's okay because I'm only getting $100 here . . . but, I'm wondering where I'll be staying? I mean . . . accommodation?"

"The Army supplies living quarters for its civilian personnel. They're old American Army barrack buildings, but they're comfortable. Hot and cold running water, telephones, oil heat. You'll eat in the consolidated mess hall. Thirty-five dollars a month for rations and quarters. You'll love the North."

He explained that a new Army command had been created especially for the arduous task of maintaining the Alaska Highway — a command called the Northwest Highway System.

"You'll hear that name a lot. *Northwest Highway System* . . . a thousand people work under that banner from Dawson Creek to the Alaska border. You'll be a clerk . . . filing, typing."

A new adventure spread before me. I felt a warm glow all over. What an opportunity, I told myself, and I was only seventeen. The comfortable living quarters especially pleased me. Deep inside I was not a true pioneer. I wanted my comfort and yet wanted to experience pioneer life, too. I did not know then that the Yukon would forge me into a tough Sourdough in the short span of three months.

Chapter 3

The hum of the Dakota aircraft had a lulling effect. I relaxed in the double seat I occupied all by myself, and remembered that, for a high school project two years before, I'd chosen to do an essay on the building of the Alaska Highway. My research had pointed out that in a diplomatic note signed by Franklin D. Roosevelt, president of the United States, and William Lyon Mackenzie King, prime minister of Canada, Roosevelt had promised to maintain the part of the Alaska Highway that lay in Canada until six months after the end of the war or the cessation of hostilities. It was now just a year since V-J Day, when World War II had come to an end. I wondered what would be the fate of 1,221 miles of the famous road. There had been articles in Alberta newspapers saying that people in Alaska were worried about this unsettled method of maintaining a road that was their only overland link with the continental United States.

The Canadian Pacific Airlines plane I was on had left Edmonton at midnight on a scheduled flight to Fairbanks. I was disappointed that the black night would not permit me to see any part of the historic gravel road that curved through five mountain ranges.

My father had had mixed feelings about my going to the Far North. "You're so young, and it's so far away," he said sadly as we'd said our goodbyes a short time before in the terminal at the Edmonton airport.

"But . . . think of all the adventures I'll be able to write about. Remember? You said Canadian history isn't dull?"

He'd brightened on that note. "Find out about that valley where aircraft are rotting away . . . and . . . and say 'hi' to Tim Condon for me. I'll send up your skis and your radio with Ralph."

We'd parted, misty-eyed on that reference to Ralph Oakes, one of several pilots flying the CP route to Alaska.

I had not seen Tim for a couple of months, and I wondered where he was. He seemed to pop up at the oddest places at the oddest times. Once he had paged me at the Corona Hotel in Edmonton when I had been covering a businessmen's conven-

Handshake between Major Bernard Zhon, 6th Service Cmd., (left), and Lt. Col. J.R.B. Jones, RCE, marks transfer of the Alaska Highway to the Canadian Army for maintenance, in a ceremony held on April 1, 1946, in Whitehorse, Y.T.
Photo by James Quong.

tion. Another time, just two months earlier, he had trailed me into a coffee shop on Jasper Avenue where *Edmonton Bulletin* reporters hung out. He said then that he was stationed at Watson Lake, about 300 miles south of Whitehorse, but his old Norseman plane was busy probing into the remotest corners of the Yukon. He had just flown into an Eskimo village on the rim of the Arctic where people were dying of starvation.

"The seal hunt had been poor, and hundreds of reindeer herds had succumbed to disease. Those people were skin and bones, and the kids, Gawd . . . the kids were pathetic. I made three flights in . . . once with a doctor and medication, and twice with grub."

As the Dak sliced through the black skies, I decided that I'd have to contact Tim, learn more about his adventures. My thoughts

At the United States-to-Canada transfer ceremony in 1946, members of the official party pass in review to take their seats on the platform. Identifiable are Col. C.M. Clifford, commanding officer of the U.S. Army Service Forces in Northwest Canada, escorting American Ambassador to Canada Roy Atherton. Following is Gen. A.G.L. McNaughton with Brig. Geoffrey Walsh, newly appointed commanding officer of the Northwest Highway System, acting as escort. Behind Brigadier Walsh may by seen Maj. Gen. G.V. Henry, U.S. military member of the Joint Defence Board, and Maj. Gen. W.N. Hoge, the first American Military Commander of the Alaska Highway Construction Forces (later performing brilliant service in forcing the German armies back across the Rhine). Also identifiable in the picture is Brig. Gen. Dale V. Gaffney, commanding officer of the Alaska Division, U.S. Army Air Force.

Photo by James Quong.

*With Scottish pipers in the lead, this parade was part of the
ceremony transferring the Alaska Highway from control of
the U.S. government to full control of the Canadian
government on April 1, 1946.*

Photo by James Quong.

14

Major L.N. VanNort, C.O. of the 843rd Signal Service
Battalion, U.S. Army (left), *congratulates Squadron-Leader*
W.W. Creegan, RCAF, as the control of 1700 miles of
telephone and teletype lines are passed from the U.S. Army
to the RCAF, on April 1, 1946.
Photo by James Quong.

were interrupted by the stewardess who had escorted a young woman from the front of the plane to the back to sit with me.

"You two are the only passengers scheduled for Whitehorse, and I thought you should know one another," she said sweetly. "Anne Peterson . . . meet Hope Morritt."

Anne gave me a tight little smile, and quietly sat down in the seat beside me. She had a long, thin face and attractive hazel eyes, and she was very pregnant.

"Where do you come from, Anne?" I asked, trying to start a conversation.

"Halifax," she answered, without looking my way.

There was an awkward pause.

"Have you ever been to Whitehorse?"

15

She shook her head.

"I guess we're both in the same boat," I said, digging out of my purse the sheet of instructions that were given to me the day before at the Army Personnel Office in Edmonton. "This says I'm to work for a Major Gibson . . . no initials. He's officer in charge of Service Corps. When I arrive in Whitehorse, I'm to report at the Canadian Army Orderly Room, and Canadian is underlined."

I waited for Anne to make a comment, but there was none. I struggled on. "This paper also says that the Army personnel officer will meet me at the airport."

Again, without looking my way, she said quietly, "My husband, Ian, is going to meet me. He's a corporal in the Army." There was a pause, then with more determination, she added, "I didn't want him to come up here to this . . . this no-man's land . . . but when you're in the Army, you have to do what you're told."

I felt sorry for her. I was excited about this big adventure. She felt threatened.

Silence fell between us. The aircraft landed briefly at Fort St.

Lights glinting, Whitehorse of 1948 sits below the Air Force Hill. The Air Force Hill road descended steeply from the air base to the main street of the town. Because of earth slides and difficulty of maintenance, the road eventually was abandoned; only traces remain. Below the hill are the U.S. Army barracks, built by the United States government in 1942 and long-since torn down.
Photo by James Quong.

John and Fort Nelson. When it approached the runway over Watson Lake, I could see the gray outline of the water, and I thought of Tim. Would he be here, asleep in his bunk, unaware that I was on my way North? Or was he off on a mission to a distant settlement on the edge of the tundra? I remembered a letter he had written to me when he first went to Watson.

"This lake has its ghost planes . . . Airocobras, a Sea Fury, Dakota, Lincoln . . . all wrecks, that, if they could talk, could tell their own story of human drama. The Dak, a U.S. Army Air Force plane, made a forced landing on a deserted bridge. Pilot and co-pilot were killed."

Finally, after a long, tiresome flight, we landed at Whitehorse. My watch said six o'clock. It was a dark morning, except for moments when a white moon skidded out from behind gunmetal gray clouds. There was a dusting of snow on the ground. Everything looked bleak . . . the frozen ground, sparse snow, the cold, dull terminal. There was nobody at the airport to meet us. I felt an acute loneliness sweep over me, and I thought Anne was going to burst into tears.

"Look, maybe Ian didn't know you were on this flight. Messages get mixed up. Cheer up. We'll find him," I said, trying to sound optimistic. A cabbie opened the door to the terminal.

"Taxi?"

"Sure," I said, happy to see an inhabitant in this foreboding land.

When we were tucked safely inside the rattly old car, I asked him if he knew where the Canadian Army Orderly Room was located. He said he did, and I told him to take us there pronto. He began to whistle a happy, lilting tune.

"My name's Sam," he hollered above the noise of the motor, then he maneuvered the car down a precarious hill that gave us a panoramic view of the lights of Whitehorse sparkling in the pre-dawn darkness. It was a view I would enjoy often, looking from the Air Force Hill toward the river where the main part of the town hugged the valley floor. At the bottom of the hill, Sam made a right-hand turn by a squat corner building marked "Klondyke Cafe."

The moon came out, and in the silvery light I saw row after row of Army barrack buildings. They looked deserted. An odd street light caught a glint of snow as it lay in patches on the ground.

"These are the Army diggin's," hollered Sam, indicating the drab buildings. He pulled to a stop in front of one building at the far end of the line. The moonlight illuminated a sign on the front: *Orderly Room — U.S. Army Engineers.*

The building was a short, low hut with a door in the centre and a square wooden landing with two steps leading up to it. The door was open. Papers lay scattered around the doorway and on the landing.

"I want the *Canadian* Army Orderly Room, Sam," I said, unable to hide the exasperation in my voice.

"Ain't this it?"

"This says U.S. Army Engineers."

"What's the diff?"

I sighed. "The U.S. Army is not the same as the Canadian Army, and also . . . the U.S. Army's gone."

"Where?" He turned around in startled amazement and faced me.

"Back to the States."

"When?"

"About eight months ago. Where've you been?"

"Right here. Honest t' God. I was born here . . . lived here all my life."

"Sam . . . you mean to tell me that I, living in Edmonton 1,500 miles away, knew that the Americans had left the Yukon, but you, living right here, didn't know?"

He lifted his peaked hat from his head and smoothed his hair with the palm of his hand.

"Sounds nuts, don't it?"

"Yeah. How come?"

"I dunno. We liked the Americans, don't get me wrong . . . but thousands came. It was like an invasion . . ."

"And you resented them."

"Yeah. Kind of."

"Even though they brought a road and prosperity?"

"Yeah. But, it was a two-way street. See . . . the Americans kept their distance. Like . . . we were two separate towns, livin' side by side."

"And when one evacuated?"

"Well . . . we just didn't know about it. After all . . . the huts are still here." He motioned toward the deserted barrack buildings.

"But surely you read the papers, Sam?"

"Naw. We only got a weekly here that's called the *Whitehorse Star*. It ain't no good."

For a brief moment I tried to assimilate all this information. I could understand how people who called a land their own would carry on a love-hate relationship with intruders, but did they *all* do this, or only a few people like Sam? And . . . if the love-hate

An unpaved street ran in front of the three-story inn and the Whitehorse Inn Cafe, where Hope had her first meal in the Yukon.
Photo courtesy Hare Collection/Yukon Archives.

The original Regina Hotel in 1948 was a homey place with a small dining room. Meals were served on attractive square tables covered with checkered cotton tablecloths.
Photo by James Quong.

*The legendary kee bird, said to fly through northern skies
in the depths of winter screaming "Kee . . . kee . . . keerist
but it's cold," was put on a crest by an enterprising soldier.
The thick felt kee bird badge became the emblem of the
Northwest Highway System of the Canadian Army. The kee
bird flew on sports jackets, coats, long johns and other
items of apparel.*

Photo by Gwen Walker, Sarnia, Ontario.

relationship was true, would it spill over to embrace the Canadian Army? Well . . . I'd find out soon, certainly in the next year. In the meantime, the here and now weighed heavily.

"Drive around once again, Sam, and go slowly," I asked. "Maybe we can see a light, something that will indicate life."

There was nothing . . . just row after row of long barrack buildings hugging shadows of the night. Finally, I gave up.

"Is there a hotel in this wild town?"

"Sure, The Whitehorse Inn. Or you could try the Regina."

"Would you like to share a hotel room with me?" I asked Anne.

"What else is there t' do?"

"Well, we could walk the streets, if there are any streets."

She turned a peaked face toward me, and her mouth puckered into a quiver. I turned back to Sam. "Take us to the inn, please."

He made a turn by the Klondyke Cafe and followed the wide, gravel road. A big, dancing sign of a kee bird advertised a jewelry store. The kee bird is a legendary bird of the Far North who, according to story, often fills the winter skies with his anguished cry, "Kee . . . kee . . . kee-rist but it's cold."

Street lights threw a glow across the facade of frontierlike shops. Sam stopped in front of a three-storey frame building. Above the wide front doors an interesting sign depicted a wild horse. The horse's mane flowed. Its hooves pounded. Giant letters proclaimed the building to be the Whitehorse Inn.

The foyer was warm, well-furnished. The desk clerk was friendly. It was 6:40 a.m. when she led us up a wide stairway to the first-floor room with two single beds. We couldn't lock the heavy wooden door. We couldn't even shut it properly. It seemed to be the wrong door for that doorway. Anne propped a plain wooden chair against the door and sank into one of the beds.

"I'm so tired, but I have to find Ian. I . . . I just can't go on without him," she said in a whimpering voice.

"Try to rest," I told her. "You need rest."

I fell on top of the other comfortable-looking box-spring bed. A weariness was seeping into my bones that threatened to erase all worry about where the Canadian Army Orderly Room was.

WHITEHORSE

1. Airport
2. Airport Hill Road
3. Main Street
4. White Pass Depot
5. Whitehorse Inn
6. Softball Park
7. Army Compound —
   barracks, admin offices, etc.
8. Dowell Area
9. Whiskey Flats
10. Refinery Area
11. Taylor & Drury and Northern
    Commercial Company stores
12. Squatters' shacks
13. Army Hospital
14. Army Mess
15. RCMP Jail
16. Canadian Army Headquarters
    and Orderly Room
17. Klondyke Cafe
18. Old Log Church
19. T.C. Richard's house
20. Sternwheelers on the river
21. 200 ft. escarpment
22. Army brigadier's residence
23. Sergeants' Mess
24. Barracks 47
25. Officers' Mess

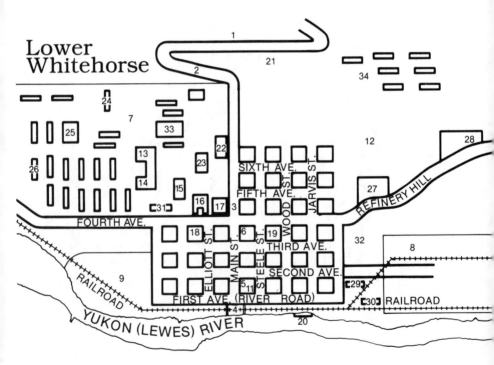

26. Barracks 17
27. Army Power Plant
28. Indian Cemetery
29. Beached river boats
30. Beached river boats
31. Army PX and Library
32. Indian settlement
33. Army Skating Rink
34. Living quarters, RCAF
35. Army Radio Station
36. U.S. Army Engineers office, warehouse and machine shop

37. Cemesto (bungalow) living quarters for officers and NCOs
38. Army living quarters for NCOs and lower ranks
39. Roads — un-named
40. Sergeants' Mess — built in 1949
41. Living quarters for a few RCAF and Signal Corps personnel

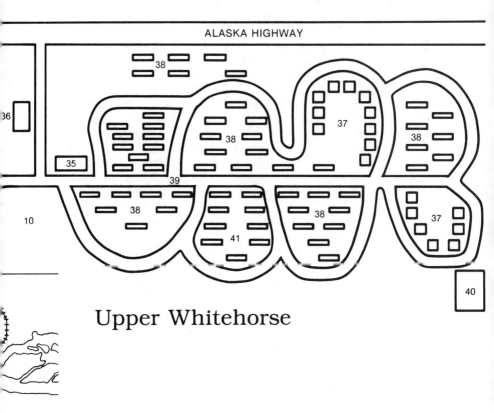

Upper Whitehorse

Chapter 4

Something hissed in the dark. I was sticky hot. The quilt on the bed was damp where I lay. The lamp on the bedside table had been on when I went to bed. I remembered that I had felt less nervous leaving the lamp on. Now, half groggy from the heat, I wondered who had turned it off. I reached over, touched the switch, and the room was bathed in a mellow glow.

Anne's bed was empty, the bedspread still rumpled where she had slept. I rose, walked around the room. Her suitcases were gone. Apparently she had found Ian, or he had found her, and they hadn't bothered to tell me they were leaving. I felt rejected, lonely. I went to the window. A steam radiator hissed and thumped under the window sill. The room was like a sauna. I opened the blind. A pale fuschia sun rose, painting the sky with an attractive blush above the hills. I looked out on rooftops that sparkled pink in the dawn-tinted frost. My watch said 7:30 a.m. I'd slept all day and all night. I dressed hurriedly and went downstairs where a dining room opened off the lobby of the inn. In a corner of the dining room, a middle-aged woman operated a switchboard.

"Can you tell me how to get to the Canadian Army Orderly Room?" I asked her.

"Well . . . the Army barracks are located . . ." She paused when she saw me shake my head. "I've been there."

She checked a phone list on the wall of her small enclosure. "I have a listing for the American Army, but nothing for the Canadians?" She looked questioningly at me.

"Maybe the American number will get the Canadians," I said, feeling helpless.

"You're new, aren't you?"

I nodded. "Arrived yesterday to work for the Canadian Army."

She laughed. "Look, honey, a whole damn Army couldn't possibly get lost up here. Have you had breakfast?"

"No."

"Well, why don't you sit down and have breakfast, and I'll

24

phone around. By the time you've finished your first cup of coffee, I'll have directions on how to get to that orderly room."

I smiled, relieved. As I ate breakfast, I spread out on the table a copy of the *Toronto Globe and Mail* that the stewardess had given to me on the airplane. There were headlines about world powers meeting at Lake Success, New York: "A British proposal to link consideration of a public report on the number of Allied troops in foreign countries with the general question of disarmament, was rejected today by Soviet foreign minister Molotov."

The veil of secrecy under which the Russians operated made me feel uneasy. I would soon discover that everybody from the brigadier to the youngest private in the Northwest Highway System felt the same uneasiness about Russia.

Another headline precluded thoughts about the USSR: "Butter ration may survive winter."

As I read, it was clear that there would not be another cut in the existing six-ounce allotment per person, per week of butter. This did not apply to the Yukon nor the Northwest Territories, which were exempt from all wartime rations.

The switchboard operator beckoned to me when I had finished my meal. She handed me a slip of paper with specific instructions on how to get to the orderly room.

"It's next door to the Klondyke Cafe, honey. Know where that is?"

"The Klondyke?" I said, surprised, remembering that Sam had driven in front of and around that area several times the morning I had arrived.

"I was told that the orderly room is set back, off the road. A big flagpole stands in front of the building, and the flag . . . get this, honey . . . the flag is the Union Jack. Don't you think it's damn well time we had a flag of our own?"

"Damn right," I said. "And thanks a million for your help."

A crisp wind, laden with a tinge of frost, stung my face as I headed toward the Klondyke. The sun was hazy, cold. I walked on the north side of Main Street, facing the distant hill that looked as if somebody had taken a knife and sliced the top off. On this flat plateau, beyond my view, were the sprawling runways and barrack buildings that made up the airport. As I looked along the wide, gravel main street, I could see where the road curved off at the far end, slanting up the hill and turning sharply at the top to join the airport road that ran along the edge of the high bluff. This was the road and hill Sam had driven us down after our arrival early Sunday morning. The hillside road had been built by the U.S. Army in 1942. Twice it had been wiped out by rockslides and rebuilt.

I passed a number of small, frontier-style shops, including a dress shop with modern fashions shown in the window, then came to a wide-open area that looked like a ball diamond. It was flanked by Fourth Street and Main and Steele streets. I crossed the road at the corner where the Klondyke sat at Fourth and Main. Everything south of this, as far as the White Pass Railroad track, and everything extending back to the base of the airport hill, was a solid mass of Army buildings.

The flagpole was easy to spot by day, the Union Jack snapping smartly in the wind. The headquarters building was an H-shaped, low, one-storey unit made of drab, unpainted wood. The orderly room, pay corps and headquarters of various units were all located here. The brigadier, with his administrative officers and staff, had offices just off the orderly room.

I walked down a long wooden sidewalk, between two flanks of the building, to the front door. Inside, a tall, bald officer rose from behind a desk and came forward. With a friendly grin, he extended his hand. "I'm Harry Gardiner, paymaster," he said.

"I'm Hope Morritt. I arrived yesterday morning, but I couldn't find the Canadian Orderly Room. You should put up a sign and a few lights."

He explained apologetically that the wheels of government grind slowly, and that the personnel man was supposed to have met me, but on a Sunday people have a habit of sleeping in.

"However, come with me and we'll get you settled," he added.

We walked to the back of the building and entered a comfortable office. He sat down behind a neat desk and told me I'd be billeted in Barrack 17, that there were three barracks for women and living quarters near the hospital for a group of nursing sisters. The buildings had been built by the U.S. Army as temporary living quarters. I opened my purse and pulled out the paper of instructions from Edmonton.

"This says I'll be working for a Major Gibson."

He nodded. "However, first you must get settled in the barrack. I'll get somebody to take you over there."

He lifted the receiver of the phone on his desk. "Give me Messing and Billeting." Pause. "Oh Mary, Captain Gardiner here. I'd like you to come over to my office to meet a new employee."

Within minutes, a short, plump woman wearing a light brown coat and overshoes came into his office. She had short brown hair and was out of breath. "I'm Mary, Hope. Sure glad you got here. We were worried, watched for you all day yesterday."

"Well . . . I got lost," I said, a little lamely.

"Come on. I'll show you where you'll be staying."

As I rose, Gardiner said he'd ask a Service Corps driver to get my suitcases from the Whitehorse Inn and drop the baggage off at the barrack. "The driver can then pick you up and take you over to Major Gibson's office," he added.

Mary and I walked the same route that Sam had taken, but the barrack buildings looked shabbier by daylight. They were unpainted and weather-beaten. A few doors were ajar with hinges squeaking, old papers and leaves eddying about.

"You'd never believe that all these buildings were full of soldiers and civilians less than a year ago," Mary said, indicating the rows of huts.

"You were here then?"

"I've been here for three years. It was great working for the Americans, but all the fun's gone now that the Canadians have taken over."

"What fun?"

"Well, there were more people, and we had dances every night at the Army theatre. That's the big building just beyond the last barrack. You can see it from here."

In the distance I could see a large building with a rounded top like a big quonset hut.

"The civilians had a special hall of their own, about a block away, just over from the Army theatre. Both places used to hum with dances, parties, movies. Now the Canadians are threatening to close the civilian hall. They run things on a shoestring." She sighed. "Cigarettes cost more. Wages are less. I really hate it now, but it's a job."

"Well . . . if the Yanks were here today they'd be cutting back on everything, too. After all, the war *is* over."

"Yeah. Time marches on, doesn't it? But, it's hard to get used to the changes."

We'd arrived at the door of a barrack building that was marked with a big "17" near one of the entrances. We went in at one end, through a small vestibule that opened into a living room. Scatter rugs, lamps, Chesterfields and easy chairs made the place look homey.

"You can use this room anytime you want, to entertain friends," Mary said. "You're not supposed to entertain men in your room, but . . . we bend that rule a bit."

A door off the reception room led into a hallway. "These are single rooms," she said, indicating closed, numbered doors on either side. She opened one that was numbered "10," and we entered. The bleak appearance of the room startled me. There was a box spring bed, plain dresser, and, tucked away in a corner, a clothes closet.

"I had the bed made up this morning. We have a maid who does odd jobs around the women's barracks. Once a week she'll leave clean linen in your room for your bed. Also, she vacuums the hallways and reception rooms, cleans the bathrooms."

Mary saw me eyeing the bare window and single light bulb dangling from a cord in the ceiling. "We're vultures around here. When somebody moves out, we lift the good things."

"Like rugs, lamps?"

"Yeah. Keep your eye on little luxuries in the room of the next person who's going to move. It doesn't really matter what room the furniture ends up in. It's all government stuff."

"Do *you* live here . . . in Seventeen?"

"No. There are two other women's barracks . . . Forty-four and Forty-seven. I'm in Forty-four." She sighed in a nostalgic way. "When the Yanks were here there were dozens of women's barracks. All full. And the men outnumbered the women one hundred to one."

A young soldier came in and deposited my two suitcases in the room. He was a stocky lad with a moon-shaped face. "This where ya want 'em?"

"Sure. That'll do," I said.

He backed out into the hallway. "I'm t' take ya to the Dowell area."

"Where's the Dowell area?" I asked, perplexed.

Mary explained that it was an area down by the river in the north end of town, named after Dowell Construction Company that had its warehouses there in 1942. Dowell was under contract with the U.S. Army to build fifty miles of road south·of Whitehorse.

Mary turned down the ride. "I'll walk. I work near headquarters. It's not far," she said.

As we left Seventeen and approached the Army staff car, a soldier sitting in the front got out and got into the back seat.

"Can't leave this vehicle for a minute but what I get strays," said the driver.

"Watch your language," came the laughing reply from the back seat.

"Just call me Vic. I'm a private in this man's Army," said the driver, turning to me. He motioned with a thumb to the back seat. "That's Al LeClair . . . a sergeant with Service Corps."

"Just call me The Frog," said Al. "We've all gotta be crazy

t' work for the Northwest Highway System."

We laughed, but I wasn't laughing an hour later when I sat in front of Major Gibson's desk.

Hope's first home in the Yukon, Barrack 17, was occupied by women employees of the Canadian Army. In February of 1947, when this picture was taken, there was neither heat nor running water in the building. Oil for the furnaces and water for the taps had frozen during an historic cold spell. Thermometer readings dropped to 70 degrees below zero (Fahrenheit) in Whitehorse, and to 82 below zero in Snag on February 3 — the coldest temperatures ever recorded in North America.

Chapter 5

Maj. W.L.G. Gibson (nicknamed "Hoot," after the cowboy movie star of the 1920s and 1930s) was not in his office when I arrived. His secretary asked me to sit in a small outer office to wait. She seemed uneasy as the minutes ticked into an hour. She kept reassuring me that Major Gibson would be in before lunch.

While I waited, the secretary explained I'd be working for 19 Company, Royal Canadian Army Service Corps, which looked after buses, staff cars and all motor transport equipment from Dawson Creek to the Alaska border. As she spoke about the various Army units working along the highway, I began to see the magnitude of this operation to maintain a mountain road that was the longest military road in the world.

At a later date I would learn that as early as October, 1945, it was announced in Parliament that the Canadian Armed Forces would take over the Alaska Highway from the United States Armed Forces, along with the land lines of the communication system, which included the telephone lines.

Brig. Geoffrey Walsh, chief engineer for the Canadian Army, returned to Canada from overseas service in Europe in August, 1945. In November he flew to Dawson Creek, B.C., where officers of the United States Army's Northwest Service Command met him. These officers drove Walsh the length of the Alaska Highway to point out the full operation, its problems and needs. In a subsequent report to Parliament, Walsh noted the Alaska Military Highway was not self-sustaining; any Canadian organization proposed would have to make provision for administration.

Before the end of 1945, three new Royal Canadian Engineers units were authorized on the Home War Establishment, under a headquarters called Northwest Highway System to be set up in Whitehorse, Yukon Territory. The new units were as follows: Highway Maintenance Establishment, an organization to be designed for highway maintenance and to be set up in small family camps along the length of the highway; No. 17 Engineer Services and Works Company, for the maintenance and operation of accommodation and installations; and No. 1 Road Maintenance Company, for large-scale road repairs and bridge work.

Gibson's secretary explained to me that, besides Service Corps, there was a Medical Corps to operate the base hospital in Whitehorse; an Ordnance Corps to issue everything from parkas to coffee mugs; a unit of Royal Canadian Electrical and Mechanical Engineers to cover major repairs of mechanical equipment; and a Pay Corps to issue pay cheques. Operating under the Army banner was also a fire department. In that self-contained area of temporary living quarters, fire was ever on our minds.

Walsh, a tall, dark-haired man with a dark moustache and keen blue eyes, became the first commander of the Northwest Highway System (NWHS). He took up residence in Whitehorse in January, 1946.

* * *

The vastness of the NWHS was mind-boggling. I began to think that perhaps I should have stayed at home. When Major Gibson finally arrived and I was ushered in to see him, I was more apprehensive about the job than I'd ever been. He was a middle-aged man, slightly overweight, and on this November Monday, he looked unhappy.

"Were you in the Armed Forces?" he asked me.

"No."

"Are you a bookkeeper?"

"No."

There was an uneasy quiet, then he told me that he didn't know what the personnel officer in Edmonton was doing. "I asked him for a bookkeeper who's been in one of the Armed Forces."

I explained that bookkeeping was not that difficult and I was sure I'd learn quickly. He shook his head and told me he didn't want me to work for him.

The Army had paid for my flight to Whitehorse with the stipulation that if I didn't like the work or the people with whom I worked, I'd pay for my own transportation out. However, nothing had been said about Whitehorse not liking me. As I sat there, feeling numb, I wondered what to do. My mind whirled in confusion for a moment, then I remembered that I'd come North to follow a dream and see an eerie valley where World War II bombers rotted away. Certainly this one little rejection would not spell the end to this dream. Without saying a word, I stood tall, turned and walked out.

I caught up with Captain Gardiner in the pay office, just as he was preparing to go to lunch.

"Major Gibson and I didn't hit it off. He wants an ex-service person and a bookkeeper," I said.

Gardiner toyed with a paperweight on his desk. Then, after a moment of thought, he said: "We need workers of your calibre in the Yukon. We prefer people who've had experience in one of the services. It's just easier for *them*, that's all, but people like that aren't easy to find. Many ex-servicemen want to get away from mess hall meals, regimentation. Believe me, we're happy that civilians like you are answering our call for help."

I sat back feeling relieved.

"Look, Captain MacKay, Reemee workshop, is desperately in need of help. How would you like to work for Mac?"

"I'll give it a try."

"He's a big, lean, friendly guy. I think you and Mac will get along like two cogs in a wheel."

(Later, I learned the Royal Canadian Electrical and Mechanical Engineers were called "Reemee" — a take-off from the old British corps called Royal Electrical and Mechanical Engineers, which the British Tommy fondly nicknamed "Reemee." The Canadian abbreviation RCEME designated the mechanics, welders, electricians and blacksmiths who struggled to keep machinery and equipment in first-class running order.)

Gardiner picked up the phone and within seconds had MacKay on the other end of the line. "Look, Mac . . . I have a new employee here who could help you out in the office while your secretary's away."

"Send her over right after lunch. My paperwork's stacked up like you wouldn't believe."

The words vibrated through the telephone line and spilled over in a metallic burst of enthusiasm. Gardiner smiled as he put the phone back in its cradle. He explained that lunch was then being served in the consolidated mess hall. He went home to eat, but, if I followed the crowd, I'd find the mess hall. A Service Corps driver would pick me up after lunch and take me to the Reemee workshop in the Dowell area.

I followed the crowd — a mingling of soldiers and civilians — and ended up in a corridor where the smell of freshly baked bread and sizzling steaks was inviting. A small woman with a pixielike face and bright brown eyes suddenly confronted me.

"You're the new secretary. Come with me. I'll introduce you to some of the other women who work for the Army . . . and some of the men, too. We're all a friendly bunch. You'll like it here. I'm

32

Leona Hughes. Just call me 'Tudy', " she said in a rush of words.

I followed her into a huge dining area which was brightly lit with overhead lights. There were rows of white tables to the right and left, and an aisle between them. We walked halfway down and sat at a table that was quickly filling up with men and women. Tudy sat across from me.

"You help yourself here, but first . . . we turn over our plates," she said, giggling, as she turned over the dinner plate that was placed bottom-up on the table. People passed along a large, steaming bowl of stew and platefuls of freshly baked bread cut in lumberjack slices. Tudy introduced me to others at the table while we ate. A shy yet friendly man in his early thirties sat next to me.

"That's Wendell Williams on your right. He's with engineers . . . but don't hold that against him," Tudy said, with another nervous giggle.

"Where will you be working?" asked Wendell, ignoring Tudy's joke.

"For Mac MacKay."

"Hey, that's just across the road from where I hang out at Seventeen Works."

"Good. I'll be seeing you now and again, then."

"You'll be using their bathroom. The Reemee one is still frozen from last winter," Tudy laughed, chewing on a mouthful.

At that moment Wendell stabbed a piece of meat with his fork and it slithered off his plate with missilelike speed, ending up in my lap.

"Gawd . . . I'm sorry," he said, shoving his chair back quickly, standing, looking pale as he handed me two large paper serviettes.

"It's all right." I forced a laugh. "It was just an accident . . ."

A dark stain had seeped into the wool of my gray skirt. When Wendell saw the stain, he threw his serviette on the table.

"Damn," he exclaimed, a pale pink blush coloring his face and travelling in waves up to his hair line. "Damn."

He turned and stalked angrily out of the mess hall.

Chapter 6

Capt. Magnus D. "Mac" MacKay was a tall, bony man with an angular face that lit up easily in a wide grin. He was sitting at his secretary's desk, struggling to type something, when I arrived. He had removed his Army tunic and rolled the sleeves of his khaki shirt up to his elbows. He rose quickly from behind the typewriter and came forward to meet me with an outstretched hand.

"I'm so glad to meet you, Hope . . . so glad." He shook my hand in a firm, warm gesture of welcome. "Let me take your coat. It's like a steambath in here."

He hung up the coat on a wooden clotheshorse in a corner of the office. "My secretary, Miss McLeod, is on vacation, and my clerk, Chuck Belyea, is out on compassionate leave. Everything happens at once."

He indicated a cluttered desk in one corner. "This is Sergeant Belyea's workbench . . . overloaded, grease-stained." He chuckled. "You'd never think it was made of good old Ontario oak, would you?"

There were nuts and bolts scattered across the desk, along with paperwork fingerprinted by grease-stained hands.

"Every vehicle that comes in for repair has to have a work order, and we're so far behind in our work orders, I wonder if we'll ever get caught up. That's what I was doing when you came in . . . struggling with those never-ending work orders."

He turned to the other wooden desk in an opposite corner of the large outer office where one door led into the workshop, another into his office, and a third led outside.

"This is where you'll be working, at McLeod's desk, but look . . . come on." He took me by an arm. "I'll show you around."

We entered his office, an inner sanctum, small, cosy, with highly polished linoleum floor and a single large window framed with dark brown drapes. The pastel walls were brightened with a few scenic pictures. His desk was neat, with books and papers arranged carefully along one edge. As we left, the phone began to ring. He closed the door on the caller.

There was a hum of machinery in the offices. It seeped through the single wall dividing offices from workshop. As we stepped out into the workshop, the noise was deafening. MacKay lifted his voice to a shout. "I've got thirty men working here." He made a broad sweep with one, long arm. "Mechanics, welders, electricians. They're great guys. You'll like them."

I had never seen such an assortment of machinery, from diesel monsters with huge, craning necks to gas-powered automobiles. A big overhead lift juggled to put a cab back into place. Sparks flew as a hooded welder held torch to steel.

"I could use a shop twice this big . . . three times, really. We do all major repairs for the northern section of the highway . . . to the Alaska border. Fort Nelson takes care of the south."

We were walking through the shop, and, although many of the men were bent over, their heads down, I felt they were studying me carefully, wondering who the new woman was, and where she would fit in to the establishment. At the far end, in a corner of the shop, a blacksmith's forge glowed crimson. A stocky, balding man wearing gloves and an asbestos apron paused as he held two strands of red-hot metal in the grip of tongs over the coals.

"This is Sinc Dunnett, the best damn blacksmith in this man's Army," yelled MacKay.

Sinc smiled, pleased, every other tooth missing.

"Sinc can brew the best coffee in the Yukon."

"Thanks, Captain," yelled Sinc.

I didn't know the significance of the coffee statement until later in the week.

We went back to the office. In spite of the piled-up work orders, MacKay was in a mood to talk. He told me that he managed the radio station — CFWH — which the Canadian Army had inherited from the Americans. I had not heard about a radio station.

"The Americans had a full-time staff operating the radio station. We're working on a peacetime budget, and a helluva poor one at that, so we can't pay our personnel."

"You mean they're volunteers?" I asked.

He nodded. "Volunteer announcers, electricians, clerks. Right now the headquarters staff is cataloguing thousands of records. We go on the air every night from six o'clock to midnight."

He told me that he had great plans for radio in Whitehorse. Hockey was big and he hoped to broadcast the games from the hangar at the airbase.

"Hockey night in Whitehorse with Mac MacKay?" He chuckled again. "Look . . . I know you're just getting settled now, Hope . . .

35

but maybe you'd think about joining us as a volunteer announcer?"

I was pleased. Radio work would be something to do in my spare time. I told him I'd think about it.

The workshop door opened with a burst and a middle-aged man in Army fatigues hurried in. He gave MacKay a fistful of papers.

"This is Ed Ellik, Hope. His bark's worse than his bite."

Ed nodded gruffly, then turned to the captain. "Sir, we're desperate for work orders."

"I know, I know." MacKay slid off the edge of the desk. "We're going to work at that right now."

The captain and I struggled with work orders for the rest of the afternoon. Every piece of equipment had a DND (Department of National Defence) number, which had to be typed on the order, along with the unit to which the equipment belonged and the repair work required. The hours melted so quickly that I was surprised when the workshop whistle announced 5 p.m. quitting time.

"I won't be here for two weeks, starting tomorrow. I have to go to Fort Nelson. However, Ed will help you with the paperwork. You start at eight in the morning, have an hour for lunch and finish at five."

As we struggled into coats he told me he'd drive me over to Seventeen. "There's a bus, but it's usually overcrowded."

* * *

Dinner at the mess hall was uneventful, and later, in my room, I emptied my suitcases, hung up clothes in the closet, folded things into drawers. My dad had promised to send up my trunk by bus. It wouldn't arrive for two weeks. When I had finished these chores, I stretched out on the bed to do some reading. An hour later the door burst open and Leona Hughes — Tudy, whom I had met in the mess hall — bounced in. She stared in horror at the bare window.

"You can't leave your window like that."

"Why?"

"Because there are peeping Toms around."

I shrugged. "So . . . they won't come through the glass."

"They might," she said, and left on the run. After a few minutes she returned with a chair and reams of newspapers. Within minutes she'd taped newspapers across the window.

"It's very kind of you to do this, Tudy, but really . . . I didn't mind the window the way it was."

36

"You're very naive. I can see you're going to need a big sister," she said, and left.

She was all of four feet, ten inches in height. I laughed at the big sister reference, put out the light and crawled into bed.

Chapter 7

An Army private in a jeep delivered mail to all offices twice a day. My "in" basket filled quickly with requests for month-end reports. One memo, from the Royal Canadian Electrical and Mechanical Engineers Headquarters in Ottawa, asked that year-end activity reports be prepared in February. The Canadian Army's first year on the Alaska Highway was nearly over. I wondered if the interesting human element of that first, pioneer year would be buried under miles of paperwork and statistics.

With Ed Ellik's help, I typed out a dozen month-end reports while I whittled away at the ever-increasing work orders. One report, however, baffled me — a Vehicle Dead Line Report. I couldn't find the file with previous Dead Line reports, nor could I find the Dead Line. Finally, Ed suggested that we go outside where he would show me the Dead Line. Bundled up in parkas and gloves, we walked up and down and around the elusive "Dead Line" — a long row of equipment waiting for parts and time in the shop for repairs. While I wrote, Ed called off the name of each unit of equipment, the DND number, the Army corps or RCAF unit to which it belonged. When I had finished typing out the report, Ed looked it over, sighed and said, "That's probably the most accurate Dead Line report that headquarters'll ever get."

I learned later from MacKay that parts for equipment were difficult to obtain, because equipment inherited from the U.S. Army was outdated. Suppliers in the States were slow to send orders, and often parts were not being manufactured anymore. The men who graded the highway, built bridges and culverts, took out dangerous hills — these men became skilled at improvising when they needed parts for machinery. And often, they had to rob one piece of machinery to get another one going.

Brig. Geoff Walsh, at a later date, said, "Our biggest problem in 1946 to 1948 was that we operated worn-out equipment inherited from the U.S. Army, and parts were hard to come by."

One afternoon, three weeks after I had begun working for 16 Company RCEME, MacKay came in, his face red, his arms flailing

38

Heavy equipment — much of it left by the Americans and difficult to repair — digs ditches along the Alaska Highway during the summer of 1947.

the air. "Somebody's been stripping our Dead Line again. One of these days I'm gonna fill him with buckshot."

I learned quickly that the Reemee Dead Line was a hot issue.

* * *

Ed came into the office one morning with a metal coffeepot full of water and fresh coffee grains. He told me to come with him and he'd show me how to get a quick brew. I followed him through the shop. He stopped at the blacksmith's forge, handed the pot to Sinc, who clipped the metal tongs to the handle, extended the pot over the hot coals, and in a few seconds handed the pot back to Ed. I could smell the mellow aroma of the freshly brewed coffee as we walked back to the office. Ed took mugs out of a cupboard, along with sugar and milk. There was an electric percolator, but it took a long time to perk; its coffee didn't have the rich taste of the forge-brewed.

* * *

My biggest problem in those early weeks at the shop was learning to spell the names of the thousands of pieces of equipment and tools. Lima cranes, four-wheel-drive weapons carriers, Landis crankshaft grinders, vulcanizers, oxyacetylene welding units, valve refacing machines, D7 Cardwell Cat cranes . . . all these terms were foreign to me. Then, one afternoon a "mechanical cow" appeared on a work order, and I thought somebody was playing a joke. With tongue in cheek, I asked the captain, "What's with this mechanical cow?"

"Damn thing's a nuisance . . . big bag of nuts an' bolts, like an overgrown washing machine. Always broken down."

"You mean it's for real?"

"You bet. Turns out that stuff in the big pitchers at the mess hall, except when it's not workin' right, the milk goes lumpy."

The "cow" broke down often, and it was a priority job when it came to Reemee to be fixed. We envied the RCAF personnel who had fresh milk flown in daily from Edmonton. We often wondered what ambitious pioneer would bring a herd of cows to the Yukon.

At a later date I capitalized on this situation and wrote a radio play about a fictitious couple who took a herd of dairy cows to rugged land just south of Whitehorse. The play was presented on a CBC network program called "Summerfallow." It was appropriately titled: "There Are Hardships That Nobody Reckons."

**

One afternoon, after I'd been working at the shop for a month, the back door to the office opened. A cold wind slithered in under the desk. I felt its icy touch on my ankles. A short, stocky man wearing a khaki parka, Army peaked hat, khaki pants and big flight boots came in. MacKay, thumbing through files, turned and gave a smart salute.

"Afternoon, sir. Helluva day."

"It's brewing up a storm, Captain."

"Sure is. Say . . . Hope Morritt, I'd like you to meet Major Blatchford, senior electrical and mechanical engineer."

The major stepped forward and shook my hand. "You're doing a great job while Belyea and McLeod are away. We sure do appreciate your help."

"Thank you," I murmured.

"And when Belyea and McLeod come back, I want you to work for me."

I was too surprised to say anything. I knew that the workshop clerk and secretary would be back the following week, and I'd wondered what I would do then.

MacKay had mentioned Blatchford many times. Also, all our reports had to be sent, through the mail, to the Senior EME. I had thought he'd be a tall, domineering man. I was surprised to find he was short and friendly.

He turned to MacKay. "I'm not staying. Just came over to tell you that I know the culprits who've been stripping our Dead Line."

"Engineers?"

"Right. Number One Road. Major Lowatt-Fraser's going to hear from me. I'm going to post sentries over there." He pointed in the direction of the long Dead Line of vehicles. "With machine guns."

He turned to go. "See you Monday, Hope . . . at my office, nine o'clock."

* * *

"I'm glad you're staying with Reemee. You'll like Blatchford," said MacKay, who then disappeared into his office to tackle a full in-basket for the afternoon. I searched through the files and found a report I'd read while orienting myself on the work at Reemee. It was a memo, Army file No. 631-52-3, listing the pioneer Canadian officers of the NWHS who'd met, September 10, 1946, to discuss inter-service responsibilities with the RCAF. The meeting was held in Brigadier Walsh's office in Whitehorse.

These Army and Air Force officers defined, under terms of the take-over, the functions of the NWHS and the Northwest Staging Route. The Army would supply maintenance of the highway, maintenance of access roads to airfields and repeater stations (for telephone lines), maintenance of roads to emergency flight strips located along the highway, and freight transit along the road.

Air Force officers defined the functions of the RCAF. They would be responsible for air transport, the maintenance and operation of the airports and the telephone lines.

My eyes travelled down the list of NWHS officers present at that meeting: Brigadier Walsh; Maj. L.E. Sarantos, district adjutant attorney and quartermaster general; Maj. William Akerley, senior highway superintendent; Maj. W.L.G. Gibson; Maj. D. Maunsell, senior medical officer; Capt. R.G. Gillespie, officer commanding, 17 Works Company, RCE; and Maj. James Walker Blatchford.

Blatchford's service records showed a distinguished military career. He had been awarded the Commander-in-Chief 21 Army

Group Certificate for good service on December 30, 1944; was mentioned in dispatches for "gallant and distinguished services in North West Europe" on April 6, 1945; was entitled to the 1939-1945 Star, the France and Germany Star, the Defence Medal, Canadian Volunteer Service Medal and Clasp, and War Medal.

When I became better acquainted with him, he often mentioned a brother, Wing Commander Howard Blatchford, DFC (Distinguished Flying Cross), who had been listed as "missing presumed dead" while on active service with the RCAF overseas during the Second World War.

Chapter 8

In the barrack, which I shared with thirteen other young women, I was the first up and out in the morning because I had to be at work earlier than most of the others. I was often the last one in, after supper in the evening, because I worked farther away from the main camp than many of the women. On an occasional morning I met one or two hurried people in the washroom of the barrack. I tried to strike up a conversation, but the attempts proved futile. Casual talk died after two or three sentences, and I was left baffled, wondering if these people with whom I lived cared about newcomers. I began to feel lonely and unaccepted. On top of this, my financial situation became bleak.

After I'd been working a week, Sgt. Mel Donaldson at Headquarters sent a sheaf of papers over to me with a note: "Please fill these out for personal documentation. Pay cheques cannot be issued until all data is recorded."

It was difficult to find time to work on these documents with the backlog of work in the office, but I struggled. Just when I thought I'd filled out all papers correctly, they'd come tumbling back in the mail, and I'd be hot on the telephone wailing, "What now?"

From the few conversations I'd had with Sergeant Donaldson, I detected that he resented having to document civilians. Once, in a frustrated mood, he wailed back at me, "We need a civilian personnel officer. I don't know why I was picked for this job."

As the weeks rolled by, my $50 — all the cash I could muster in Edmonton when I left — faded away. Christmas was coming up quickly, and not having enough money for gifts made me feel resentful toward the Army. Since this was the first time I'd been away from home, the aloneness I felt when I entered the barrack each evening was acute. My sad financial state made it worse.

I chided myself for having bought colorful cretonne curtains for my bedroom window, two scatter rugs for the floor, and a bedside lamp. These items had strained my budget, but they made the room look homier. After work each night, I closed the door

43

against the aliens around me and crawled into a novel by Pearl Buck or Edna Ferber.

One Friday night I was reading, stretched out on my bed, when the door flew open and Tudy bounced in. "Here you are, stuck away in your room again, reading," she said.

I ignored the accusation in her voice and motioned for her to sit down in an easy chair I'd borrowed from the reception room. She pretended not to understand and stood, instead, in the middle of the room, hands on her hips, frowning down at me.

"You're not going to be very popular, you know, shutting yourself away like this."

I just stared at her, and she continued nonstop. "The other women think you're stuck-up. You just come and go, back and forth to work, and when you're home you retreat to . . . to your ivory tower."

"Just a minute, Tudy . . . I've tried to make friends."

"Of whom?"

"A tall girl with blond, streaked hair."

"That's Betty Myles. We call her 'The Skunk' because of the streak . . . but she's a swell person."

"Well, I tried to talk to her, but —"

"But she said she tried to talk to you, and she found you a cold fish."

I felt annoyed. "Well, I don't care what she thinks."

"You'll be lonely if you don't make an effort to get to know the women."

"Maybe I want to be lonely, or at least alone," I retorted, angry with her for the intrusion.

"The people in this barrack are lots of fun," she said, seeming not to hear me.

"And, how do you get to know them?"

"Look, several of us are having a party tonight in Betty Myles's room, and they asked me to ask you to come."

"*They* asked you to ask me?"

"Yeah . . . the half-dozen people in there now. It's all women."

I sighed. "I just don't have anything to take to a party at this late date . . . bottle of wine, cheese. Not even a few crackers, so forget it."

"Just bring yourself. That's all we want."

I hesitated and she seemed to read my thoughts. "When you first hire on with the Army, it takes a long time before you get paid. We all went through that."

"How long?"

She paused, her brown eyes studying me, flinching a little, then

44

finally she blurted out, "Maybe . . . three months."

"What? Three months? How do they expect people to live?"

"Well . . . you don't have to worry about rations and quarters. The Army doesn't mind waiting, and whatever you owe them is taken off your first pay cheque before you ever get it. So, eating and sleeping is no problem. After that it's just smokes, clothes, an odd movie. . . ."

"And Christmas gifts."

"Look, I can loan you fifty to tide you over."

"Thanks, but no."

"Well, think about it. We've hired a civilian personnel officer. She might hurry things up."

"Really?"

"Yeah. Rena Fraser. From Edmonton. She should arrive any day now."

I thought of the troublesome documents that were still unfinished in my desk, and I felt elated that somebody would take them over and finish them for me. My life began to brighten a little.

"It's ten o'clock. Let's go to the party," she persisted.

I stood up, towering above her. "Am I okay like this?" My gabardine slacks and turtleneck sweater were a little creased, but I didn't feel like changing.

"Sure."

Betty's room looked like something from the Royal York Hotel in Toronto — soft lamps, wall-to-wall carpet, artistic prints on the pastel walls, easy chairs, and a bright satin bedspread on the bed, which was lined with cosy-looking cushions. The room was twice as big as mine. It was smoky and there was a tangy aroma of rum. Tudy introduced me to the women there.

"We're switchboard operators, nurses, secretaries . . . all working for this Northwest Highway System. Where do you fit in, Hope?" asked Betty.

"I'm a clerk, wading through an avalanche of paperwork at the Reemee shop."

They laughed, and then somebody flung out, "You're also a journalist . . . worked for the *Edmonton Bulletin* at one time?"

I was surprised that they knew that much about me.

"I worked for a daily in Edmonton," I murmured.

"Well, we don't hold that against you," Betty said. She chuckled in a deep-throated way. I thought she was attractive . . . tall, wearing a housecoat of bright blue to match her eyes, a cigarette in her fingers. She rose slowly from her half-lounging position on the bed.

45

"You're a cheechako, you know."

"A newcomer," one voice explained.

"We always initiate cheechakoes."

"Like you want me to wrestle a polar bear?"

The room erupted into laughter, and I, who was usually quite shy, was having fun. Betty held up a bottle of rum. "Overproof . . . the only stuff that won't freeze on the trail at eighty below. How about a full glass, straight?"

Betty laughed, throwing back her head, displaying even, white teeth. "We're not quite that cruel . . . six ounces, one at a time, cut with Coke."

The first overproof rum brought tears to my eyes, but the second one went down smoothly. I sat back to enjoy the talk.

"D'you guys realize it's twenty-one days to New Year's Eve?"

"Hey . . . there've been a lot of changes this year." Betty held up her glass. "The year's dying, let him die."

Glasses clinked.

"The American days are over. They'll never come back, not as we knew them."

"Yeah." Betty sighed, and there was a moment of silent recall when the room was filled with feelings of nostalgia.

"D'you think those damned Russians are gonna come this way?" Betty asked.

"They're on the march in Manchuria," said Adelaide, an American woman. "They've disarmed hundreds of thousands of captured Japanese soldiers and they've transferred Jap prisoners-of-war to Siberia."

"I really don't feel very safe. We've even built a road to pave the way for a Russian attack," Betty said.

"Would you feel safer if American troops were still here?" I asked.

"Hell yes!" they shouted, almost in unison.

There was a general sigh, and in that sigh, one could detect hidden fears. Perhaps it was the fear that prompted a tall, good-looking switchboard operator to reach for a mouth organ. "Let's sing."

Somebody took my glass and refilled it.

"There's a salmon-colored girl, who has set my heart a-whirl, and she lives up in the Yukon far away —"

We sang verse after verse of this and other songs I had never heard. The laughter and voices grew louder as the night wore into morning. Outside, a December wind howled, dumping more snow across the land, but inside, the four big oil furnaces in the hallway and reception room of the barrack belted out a hearty heat. There

46

was also a warmth in Betty's room, a rowdy sharing.

After a sixth rum, I could not rise from the chair without falling on my face. A group of women carted me into my room, put me into pajamas and shoved me into bed. Their voices were fuzzy and their faces came at me and retreated like a bad movie. I vaguely heard one of them say, as she left, "You're now a sourdough . . . one of that tough breed of men and women who came with the Yanks in '42, to build a road."

The next day I thought ten little devils were imprisoned in my head, each with a hammer, pounding to get out.

Chapter 9

The Army flooded a rink behind the headquarters building. A high board fence circled the ice and strings of lights lit up the surface like an arena.

My dad had sent up my skates along with skis and a trunk full of extra clothes and commodities. On a tingling night, when the thermometer read 20 above zero (Fahrenheit), I wandered over to the rink, sat on a bench and put on my skates. Several women were there, along with soldiers and civilians who lived in the Army compound. I found myself skating with strangers, and yet, I felt as if I'd known them for a long time. There was a common bond uniting us — the Army and a mountain road that seemed to stretch to the edge of the world. The road, in fact, was often a conversation piece. That first skating night I was introduced to a sergeant with No. 1 Road Maintenance Company, Royal Canadian Engineers. A tall, dark-haired man of about twenty-four, he had an exciting way of telling a story about the road.

"Just came up from Little Rancheria this morning. Drove all night," he said, as we drank coffee at the Klondyke, after skating.

He lit a cigarette, and I remembered that the Canadian Army was building its first steel bridge to replace wooden trestles at Little Rancheria River and Big Creek, about 300 miles south of Whitehorse.

"Drove a Sterling tractor pulling an empty pole trailer forty-five feet long. I'll be loading steel all day tomorrow t' take back t' the bridge site. . . ."

He paused again and took a long drag from his cigarette. "You wouldn't believe some of the things that happen on the road."

"Like?"

"Like early last spring, I was driving this outfit . . . the tractor and trailer . . . t' Whitehorse, comin' up for a load. Spring's bad. Creeks an' rivers swell with the spring run-off. Bridges wash away. Whole chunks o' road vanish."

"Really?"

"You never know what you'll meet, like that particular spring

48

A spring flood in 1947 washed out the work bridge (temporary bridge) at Little Rancheria (Mile 670, Alaska Highway).

A crane hoists steel for the new bridge at Little Rancheria on the Alaska Highway, in the summer of 1947.

Soldier crews put down reinforced steel prior to pouring cement on the new bridge decking at Little Rancheria.

The new Little Rancheria Bridge stands ready for Canadian Army soldiers to pour a cement pavement.

mornin' I'd noticed some rivers had flooded their banks, but the gravel on the road seemed hard enough, with good ruts in the middle . . . right down the middle like twin ribbons of steel."

"Made by cars and trucks?"

He nodded. "See . . . I came to this bridge, an' the road ruts leadin' up t' the bridge seemed t' shimmer in the early mornin' sun. I steered, careful-like, an' hit the ruts dead-on with the tractor. Once I was on the bridge, I saw that the ruts leadin' off on the other side were shinin' too. It was kinda like a mirage, a little mist risin' across the road, as if I was seein' it all in a dream."

"And you hit those ruts dead-on, too?" I asked, seeing this drama unfold like a movie.

"Yeah . . . but this is where trouble hit."

"What trouble?"

"I drove onto the road with the tractor, then my whole outfit shook an' shuddered, jerked an' spun all over the road."

"All *over* the road?"

"All over . . . and off . . . except I didn't see it go off the road 'cause I was thrown under the dash. Whew." He ran a sleeve of his tunic across his forehead to wipe off the perspiration that was coming back with the telling. "When we finally stopped rolling, I couldn't believe my eyes. The trailer was five hundred feet *ahead* of me."

"Ahead?"

"Yes. And crosswise in the road. But . . . back at the bridge, I saw that the spring runoff had eaten out all the gravel and fill around the bridge abutment on the one side."

"And the ruts were all that were left of the road?"

"Exactly. The tractor held up okay, but the trailer didn't." He shook his head sadly. "If I'd had a load o' steel on that trailer, I wouldn't be talkin' t' you now."

I smiled at his vivid recall of the accident. He was a handsome man, with a striking personality, whose name was Dan Cameron. He would come into my life again.

The Klondyke was open night and day. We often sat around a pot-bellied heater that belched out a homey aroma of wood, while we listened to stories of the road.

* * *

After my initiation with the overproof rum at Betty Myles's party, people with whom I lived became friendlier. They often joined me in my room for a coffee — brewed over an electric hot plate — or talks about politics, books, or the road.

51

One evening shortly before Christmas, I had just come home after supper. I took off my coat and boots and was seated on the side of the bed trying to catch my breath when a tall, big woman with a cheerful smile appeared in my doorway.

"Hi. I'm your neighbor. Just arrived today. Have you a pair of skates I could borrow?"

"Sure, but . . ." I paused and studied her feet. They looked much bigger than mine. I dug the skates out of my closet.

"They're size seven," I said apologetically.

"That's okay. I'm a ten, but I'll double up my toes. Thanks."

She took the skates and left on the run, then Tudy bounced into my room.

"I see you met big Rena."

"Big Rena?"

"Sure. Rena Fraser. The personnel officer."

"Oh . . . is that who she was?"

"Yeah. You'll like her. She's lots of fun. Was the first regimental sergeant major in the Canadian Women's Army Corps, and, for her work with the CWAC, she was invested as a member of the British Empire."

"I *am* impressed," I said, remembering that the MBE was an award instituted in 1917 by King George V of England, to reward British and allied subjects who had rendered special services on the war front or on civvy street. A man became a "Knight" and a woman a "Dame." "Dame Rena Fraser," I contemplated. How exciting . . . like knowing a royal princess.

"Do you think she'll get my crazy documents finished in time for me to get paid for Christmas?"

"She might. She's a worker, and she's got pull."

The next evening, Rena appeared again. "Thanks for the skates," she said, depositing them on the floor.

"You're not crippled?"

"No." She sat down on the only chair in my room. "I'm struggling to get your documents in order, but . . . you and I will not get paid before Christmas."

"Damn!"

"I know. I feel like an orphan, too, but look . . . just before I left Edmonton I had a stroke of luck. Sold my piano. My mother had great hopes that I'd be a virtuoso some day, but she's resigned that some things just don't materialize."

She put an envelope on my bedside table. "I got one hundred for that old relic. Imagine . . . one hundred dollars! I'd like to split it with you . . . fifty-fifty."

"Thank you," I said with a grateful sigh. "The stores are open

Rena Fraser served as civilian personnel officer for the Northwest Highway System, a branch of the Canadian Army responsible for maintenance of the 1,200 miles of Alaska Highway that lay in Canada.

tonight. Do you think if I hurry and get gifts and mail them tomorrow, they'll arrive in Edmonton for Christmas?"

"Sure," she said warmly. "Let's go."

Chapter 10

A subdued twilight lay outside the latticed windows of the mess hall as we sat down on Christmas day for turkey dinner. Candles glowed in an assortment of colors on the fifty-odd tables. Yuletide centrepieces in green and red contrasted sharply with the white linen tablecloths. The overhead lights were dimmed while we ate.

At our table, set for eight, we were a mixed group — Rena, Betty, Tudy and I — along with three out-of-town civilians who worked for the Army, and a young soldier named Sid. Drinks had been floating around all the barracks throughout the day, but I hadn't seen anybody drunk, just mellow.

We were lingering over the last course — plum pudding — when Sid leaned my way and said, "Don't you think it's warm in here? Don't you think somebody should open a window?"

"I'm not warm, Sid."

"But . . . I'm warm," he insisted.

I looked at the windows . . . thick glass with additional storm sashes.

"The windows don't open, Sid. If you're too warm . . . maybe you could go outside for —"

"The windows don't open?" He stood, teetering a little. "We'll see." He leaned back, shadowboxing. People stared, wondering what the heck he was doing, then suddenly he thrust out a fist and put it through the double window. Glass and blood splattered all over our end of the table.

"Sid . . . look at your hand," hollered Tudy as she reached across the candles to try to help him.

"Oh," he murmured, sinking down on the chair, his florid face turning ashen as he held up the shattered hand. Blood poured down his arm, into his sleeve. I'd never seen so much blood all at once in my life.

Two soldiers from the next table jumped up, and, taking Sid by an arm on either side, helped him out of the dining room. The Military Hospital was joined to the mess hall by a main corridor.

54

Tables are set and waitresses and kitchen staff are ready for Christmas Day, 1946, inside the Candian Army mess hall in Whitehorse. Both civilian and military personnel ate their meals here.

The trio disappeared down that corridor in the direction of the hospital.

I saw Sid two days later, his hand covered in bandages.

"Happy New Year," he said with a sheepish grin.

* * *

I was glad the last day of the old year passed without bloodshed. I'd promised Mac that I'd take over at the radio station on New Year's Eve. A staff car picked me up at Barrack 17 at 5:30 p.m. Vic, the private, once again was driving.

We were silent as we drove up the refinery hill, past the Indian graveyard where spirit houses, marking the graves, looked like cold silhouettes in the night. The refinery, across the road and up the hill a little farther, lay on a flat plateau that swept toward the river. Built in 1944 as a war measure, the refinery, fed by oil from Norman Wells in the Northwest Territories, had operated for only nine months. It was closed down when World War II ended. As we drove by, it looked silent and forlorn, its cracking towers and stacks outlined against the winter sky.

Vic stopped in front of the radio station, which was located in one end of an Army hut on top of the hill.

"D'you think you could do me a favor?" he asked wistfully. "Play 'White Christmas'?"

"Sure, *if* I can find it."

The 50-watt station with call letters CFWH operated on programs sent by the U.S. Armed Forces Radio Broadcasts in Los Angeles. During the war, all the popular radio programs were recorded on one-hour discs and sent on circuit through the North Country wherever there were U.S. troops. After the war, the big discs continued to come, although all of the American troops had left.

As I unlocked the door of the radio station, I remembered that a few days earlier, during Christmas week, Whitehorse merchants had treated the operators of CFWH to coffee and Christmas cake in the small outer studio. Each of us was presented with a gold nugget silver spoon, and a spokesman for the merchants told us that this gift was a small token showing their appreciation of our efforts to bring radio programs to Whitehorse.

The station was the only set of its kind geared to supplying entertainment in the Yukon. It was also the only radio station in Canada with the transmitter located in the bathroom. We actually operated from three small rooms — an outer studio, an operations room where turntables and mikes were located, and the bathroom. We could not transmit farther than ten miles north or south on the highway.

Few people had aerials powerful enough to pick up Outside points. (The word Outside meant civilization south of the 60th parallel.) The ordinary, mantle-sized radio with a short-wave band could sometimes pick up programs in Vancouver, but the reception was never good. The northern lights and high mountain ranges gave us static and fade-in, fade-out reception from Outside.

Mac always left our broadcast schedule carefully typed on the turntable. I noted, on this last day of the old year, that my schedule included Fibber McGee and Molly, Charlie McCarthy and Edgar Bergen, and a radio theatre program — all recorded about a month before.

My first job on this night, as on a regular night, was to phone the repeater station at MacRae, ten miles south, and to ask for a telephone line to Station CKUA in Edmonton. The six o'clock news was always relayed over the telephone line. After plugging in our set to the line, I talked to the announcer in Edmonton for half a minute, then faded out on a march on my set and faded in on the news. It always amazed me when the newscaster's voice came in, loud and clear. In fact, it seemed like a miracle, and often I thought that the birth of the telephone lines that brought the voice had certainly been a miracle.

I knew that in 1942 it took the Miller Construction Co. of Indianapolis, Indiana (working for the American Army) two years to build the four-strand system. Construction began in Edmonton, with the line going from there to Grande Prairie, Dawson Creek, Whitehorse and Fairbanks. From Whitehorse, another line spurred off to the northeast to link with Norman Wells in the Northwest Territories, 600 miles away.

The whole system served a territory comparable in area to Europe — a Europe with few inhabitants. Stretching for 2,850 miles, the telephone line was one of the longest open-wire toll circuits in the world. A copper weld wire was used (a coating of copper, welded to an inner wire of steel). Between Dawson Creek and Fairbanks, 85,000 telephones poles were erected, hacked out of the Canadian bush. Twenty-eight repeater stations (also called booster stations) were built, each requiring about fifty tons of equipment. There were twenty-one channels of communications: twelve telegraph circuits, two direct-current telegraph circuits and seven talking circuits.

Although the building of this telephone system had been something to cheer about a few years before, the news on this night of December 31, 1946, was not.

Fear war in Indo-China will spread south . . . 1,088 now dead in Jap earthquake . . . Soviet orders U.S. warship out of Dairen, Manchuria . . .

After the news I was glad to put Fibber McGee on the turntable for a light touch. I turned up the speakers in the outer studio so that I could hear the program while I searched for "White Christmas." I was seated on the floor, surrounded by records, about an hour later when the outer door to the studio opened. I felt a rush of cold air, and when I turned to see who had come in, I was amazed and delighted to see Tim Condon huddled up in a parka with Air Force blue trousers tucked sloppily into over-sized flight boots. He saluted.

"How the hell are ya, kid?" He stepped over, pulled me to my feet and gave me a giant hug.

"Where have you been?" I asked.

"Never mind *me*. What about *you*?"

He took his parka off and draped it over an electric organ in one corner of the room. "I was stretched out on my bunk at the air base tonight, feeling sorry for myself. You know . . . poor pilot can't even get leave to go home for Christmas, see his ma and

57

pa, young sisters, brothers. I turned my radio on, and I couldn't believe my ears. This gentle voice came at me. 'Radio Station CFWH will continue to broadcast till midnight. Your announcer is Hope Morritt. . .' " He shook his head incredulously. "Kee-rist . . . I thought I'd left you in Edmonton three months ago."

"Okay. So I'm here. But, what are *you* doing here?"

"Brought an Eskimo woman down from the frozen tundra. She's expecting a baby and there are complications."

"And . . . you're leaving tomorrow?"

"Wrong. Day after tomorrow. Back to Watson Lake. But look . . . have you found Brad?"

"No. Where the heck does he hang out? I've looked all around Whitehorse."

"Would you like to meet him?"

"Yes. But where is he? Like . . . I haven't seen any jewelry shop with charms made from aircraft in The Valley."

"He's not easy t' find . . . tucked away, off the main drag, but . . . we're going over there tonight. I phoned him. He's expecting us."

"Tonight? I won't be finished here till midnight. Can't put the set on remote control."

"I know. I'm a night hawk, and so are you, kid, and so is Brad."

Just before midnight we found "White Christmas" with Bing Crosby as the vocalist. It was a great way to end the day.

We locked up, got into an Air Force jeep that Tim had borrowed, and drove down the hill, past the Indian graveyard and the refinery. We took a turn down Main Street toward the White Pass and Yukon Railroad station, then turned right a block before the River Road. Tim headed away from the town and into a ghettolike area.

"I hope you know you're in the sleazy part of town. We call this place Whiskey Flats," I said.

"Scared, kid?"

"No."

"You should be."

Chapter 11

The rambling trails through Whiskey Flats had no twinkling streetlights to throw a mellow glow around corners, and no moon this night to cover all with a fairylike sheen. The fifteen or twenty frame houses hugged the river. They had been built in haste in clapboard style, during the American days, to accommodate transients who followed road construction gangs. They took advantage of squatters' rights; the undeveloped land had no apparent owner. Electricity was the only utility supplied to each house. The place was dubbed "Whiskey Flats" because rumor had it that the amount of whiskey consumed at parties each week could keep one of the old paddlewheelers afloat to Dawson City (400 miles downriver) for a year.

"This is it," said Tim as he parked the jeep in front of a low, boxlike frame house.

A musty smell of wood heat met us as we stepped inside. From an inner room came the steady buzz of an electric saw.

"Hey, Brad . . . where the hell are ya?" called Tim.

The buzz stopped. A tall, well-built man with blond beard and blond, shaggy hair stepped through the doorway on the far side of the room. With two long strides he joined us and affectionately squeezed Tim's shoulder.

"Gawd! It's good t' see you."

They laughed, talked and shared private jokes for a few minutes while I studied the small room. A homemade display case standing on thick, unvarnished wooden legs met a visitor just inside the door. Leaning out from the wall at an angle, the case was rigged up on the inside with bare light bulbs. The jewelry pieces looked rich, gleaming on dark blue velvet on the bottom of the shallow case.

In contrast to this attractive display, the "shop" had a pioneer look — scuffed floor boards, spruce walls full of knots. Across the back, in bold staggered letters, was the message: "All Jewelry Hand-Crafted By Owen Bradley From The Wrecks of Aircraft In

Million Dollar Valley." Under this, an airplane propeller made of wood hugged the wall.

Rough shelves lined the room, displaying several wall crosses, daggers with wooden handles, paperweights, bookends. I was so fascinated with the overall picture that I jumped when Tim put a hand on my arm.

"Hope Morritt, I'd like you to meet Owen Bradley."

Brad's handshake was vicelike, making me wince a little in pain. I noticed he had the bluest eyes — the color of a summer sky on a cloudless day. He was rugged in an appealing, sexy way. He reminded me of a Viking sailor who would look well at the helm of a Nordic ship.

"This is a kind of workshop, where I display my wares, wait on customers." He waved his arm to indicate the room. "I might say business is lucrative. I've hired a helper, a young Indian lad who makes these." He picked up one of the daggers. "And these." He showed us a cross on the wall, made like a totem pole.

"I had a display in the Hudson's Bay store in Edmonton two months ago . . . sold everything. I was amazed that people were so interested in artwork made from planes in a ghostly valley."

"You kinda hit a mother lode, didn't you, Brad?"

"You can say that again. I *love* the money. I could be a millionaire in short order. I like the ring of that word *millionaire*. But look . . . let's go into my living quarters, have a drink, celebrate the Yule season."

He took us through a narrow room, joined to the workshop by an open doorway. Cardboard boxes full of metal pieces littered the area. A workbench at one end was lit by bright, overhead light bulbs. A large unfinished cross and bracelet lay on top of the work table. Small electric polishers and drills were scattered nearby.

He took us through another doorway that led into his kitchen-living room. A small bedroom with unmade bed could be seen at one end, and adjoining the kitchen at the other end was a bathroom, big enough for a person to turn around in, equipped with a sink, mirror and chemical toilet.

We sat in the kitchen, around a wooden table. The walls were unvarnished knotty spruce. A big wood-burning stove heated the whole place. A sink — with hand pump, counter top and cupboards above and below — was stacked with dishes.

"No running water. I've rigged up a pump for rainwater," said Brad. "That's it. My home. Not very fancy, but I'm happy."

"I didn't think you'd ever settle down like this, Brad. I mean, let's be realistic, you were a wild man overseas."

Brad laughed, showing strong white teeth. "You should talk.

60

I used to think that you thought you were immortal when you got behind the controls of a Spit."

"Those were the days, weren't they?" Tim shook his head nostalgically. "But . . . at least I'm still flying."

"Jeez . . . you can hardly compare that plodding old Norseman to a Spit."

"Maybe not. But I'm up there where I want t' be. And flying this north is no easy touch. You gotta have your wits with you, and a sixth sense, too."

Brad poured drinks — rum and Coke — passed them around, then sat down on a kitchen chair and lit a cigarette.

"I don't want t' fly again. Had my fill of that overseas . . . but you, Tim . . . you're hooked. Service was thinking of you when he wrote, 'There's a race of men who won't fit in, a race that won't stand still —' "

"Hey now . . . that's the pot calling the kettle black. You're pretty goddam restless yourself, man. You've been to Yellowknife, Fairbanks, Juneau. You've mushed dogs over a trap line, mucked for gold from here to Dawson City . . . and now you're digging for a fortune in a valley full of ghost planes."

I felt as if this was a game these two were playing — challenging one another with words — and yet they were serious, too.

"And the diggin's good . . . all kinds of metal, free for the taking, to satisfy my artistic whims and my pocket. And here," he motioned to his house and shop, "there's no rent. I only pay for electricity, get my drinking water from the river in a galvanized pail, sell my wares without worry of taxes. That pot o' gold at the end of the rainbow that we've been searching for, all these years."

Tim lit a cigarette, inhaled, then slowly exhaled. "And . . . you're going back into The Valley?"

"Damn rights. In June. Those hollow-steel propellers are tops . . . easy to work with, polish up like a mirror."

"Don't tell Uncle Sam."

Brad laughed roguishly.

"Of course . . . you and I both know, Brad, that those bombers'll never get out. The valley has strange currents that lock 'em in."

"Sure, sure," I said with skepticism, knowing that Tim flung out that statement for my benefit.

"You want to see The Valley, Hope?" Tim studied me seriously.

I sat forward and leaned across the table, studying Brad. "D'you think you'd have room for me?"

"Can you rough it? I'll rent a Junkers or Waco . . . fly in for a week?"

"Sure."

"You're on."

I felt as if I'd taken the initial step into a twilight zone that had haunted me for over a year. It was an elated feeling, my heart thumping wildly in anticipation, every nerve jumping. I heard little of the conversation from then on. My watch said seven o'clock as Tim and I stepped out into the cold, dark morning. The night had flown on wings of nostalgia, repartee and rough plans for a flight into a strange, almost supernatural valley.

"Let's have breakfast," said Tim as he parked the jeep in front of the Whitehorse Inn.

He was hanging loose, mellow from a little too much rum. We sat, hunched over the small table in the little dining room. On this first day of 1947, all places of business were closed, with one or two cafes willing to accommodate customers. Except for a waitress and one other diner, we were alone.

"Ya know, Brad's trying to kid us and himself, too, when he says he doesn't want t' fly again."

"What makes you think that?"

"I know him. He's addicted to flying. I'm not saying that the work he's doing with the bracelets and things isn't good. It is. He's quite an artist, but then, his father was a jeweller in Winnipeg several years ago. He kind of inherited the touch. Also, he's got a good thing going, but it won't last."

"You mean he'll go back to flying?"

"Yeah." Tim lit a cigarette. "There's something about being up there, away from everything and everybody . . ." He pointed to the sky overhead. "A kind of release. And . . . even when you land at remote places, there's a feeling of freedom, of not having to conform, like when I come down on isolated lakes, fish from the pontoons, build a fire on the shore, have dinner. This North Country's great. My mechanic and I often feel we're the only humans to set foot in some o' these wild, rugged places. It's like . . . like science fiction . . . the moon, stars and an old Norseman to take you there."

"What about winter?"

"I can go anywhere on skis. Once landed in a blizzard at Old Crow, and once on the Arctic Ocean to rescue Eskimo hunters adrift on an ice floe. It's like playing God, bringing food supplies, doctors, medicine, life."

"But Brad doesn't seem to like a Norseman?"

"No. That would be too slow for Brad. Wacos, Junkers, Howards . . . all too slow. He'll get back into combat some day."

"When? Where?"

Tim shrugged. "A year, two. When he's no longer hypnotized by The Valley. And where? Who knows."

"You mean he's not only addicted to flying, but combat, too?"

"Fast, fierce flying. And danger."

He sighed, eased back in his chair and was quiet a moment. "I was in love once, kid . . . in England. Gawd . . . she was beautiful. Sometimes I still dream about her." He paused, looking far away, as though seeing England again, a tender, April England. "It was exciting, electric. I wanted to make a lifetime thing of it, but she wouldn't go for it. 'I couldn't stand the competition,' she said, 'from the other woman.' "

He paused again, and in the silence that followed I felt like an outsider, looking in on a drama unfolding. After a few minutes, I dared to intrude with a whisper, "The other woman? An airplane?"

He studied me in a concentrated way, as though looking at me for the first time. "I won't let myself fall in love again." His eyes lit up with excitement, an appealing flush darkening his lean face. "I'd like to love *you* . . . take you to bed. I've thought about it, don't think I haven't . . . but there would always be the other woman."

We sat quietly, saying nothing, drinking our after-breakfast coffee. A cold, new year's dawn rose slowly, destroying a romantic glow and a quasi-divine world of yesterdays and might-have-been tomorrows.

Chapter 12

The work in Major Blatchford's office was not as challenging or as exciting as the work had been in the Reemee workshop. I missed the hordes of people who came and went at the shop, Mac's exuberance, and the coffee perked over the blacksmith's forge.

Helen Alexander, an attractive woman of thirty-nine years, was Blatchford's secretary. She, however, was ill much of the time, and not able to get to the office. Also, as senior electrical and mechanical engineer for the highway, Blatch was away often on inspection trips that took him as far north as the Alaska border, and south to Dawson Creek. The office was far too quiet and remote for my liking. It was at the end of a long barrack building where Service Corps offices also were located. At the opposite end of the building, Hoot Gibson had his office. In the spring Gibson went Outside on posting and Major D.S. Nicholson — a friendly, round-faced defenceman on the Army hockey team — became the new senior supply and transport officer of 19 Coy RCASC.

One set of windows in the rear of Blatchford's office looked out toward the river, where I could see the bulk of an old paddle-wheeler that ran the river around the turn of the century. It was rotting away, beached, propped up by two-by-fours and snowdrifts.

* * *

The years 1946 to 1950 marked a transition for the Alaska Highway. We, in Whitehorse, often heard rumors that key military figures in Ottawa wanted to liquidate the Northwest Highway System and let the road revert back to wilderness. The purchase of guns, tanks, submarines and other engines of war was more important than a remote mountain road.

The U.S. government had spent $150 million to build the Alaska Highway; Prime Minister Mackenzie King provided the right-of-way and waived customs duties on materials. After the

Early-day sternwheelers such as this one were drawn up on the beach along the waterfront at Whitehorse during the 1940s.

Photo by James Quong.

war, Canada purchased the highway from the United States for $108 million. In those postwar years, we who worked for the NWHS lived in an uneasy world. No one was certain that a quarter of a million dollars would not be tossed to the wolves and all our jobs scrapped with the quick stroke of a pen. No one was sure, either, that the Russians wouldn't attack us, coming over the roof of the world to Alaska and on down the road. Then there was nature, a sometimes deadly foe that snapped at our heels now that winter spread its hoary breath across the land.

* * *

Toward the end of January the mercury began to fall. When it hit 35 below zero (Fahrenheit) I began to take a short-cut to work, walking through an Indian village. Dogs ran in packs, shacks looked as if they would fall with a puff of wind. I liked to talk to the Indian children, who were beautiful little creatures with their shy smiles and wine-dark eyes. These people were Kutchin Indians, often referred to as "Stick" Indians, a term meaning "forest," taken from the Chinook jargon (no longer used in the Yukon).

One day, when every breath hung in the air like a starched piece of gauze, I stopped to talk to an eleven-year-old Indian child.

"It's so cold. How do you keep warm?" I asked.

She looked at her moccasined feet a moment, then said shyly, "We sleep with our dogs."

I recoiled with horror, thinking that the dogs probably had fleas and these fleas would be shared by all. But I remembered the Indian child on the morning of January 31, when I awoke in my bedroom feeling stiff and cold. Twice during the night I'd reached for extra covers, once to pull another Hudson's Bay blanket over my head, and later to unfold a down-filled comforter at the foot of the bed. As I awoke, the cold seemed to penetrate to the core of my being. I touched the switch on my bedside lamp. In the flood of light, my totem-pole thermometer came to life on the edge of the table. I noted with a start that the red band of mercury in the centre was gone. My eyes travelled up the column, then hastily down. It was at the bottom, that elusive red band, but . . . what was it doing there? I rubbed the sleep out of my eyes and looked again. It pointed to sixty degrees below zero — a Fahrenheit reading.

Suddenly my alarm sounded off. The clock usually rang with a high-pitched wail. On this particular morning it grumbled like a frigid bullfrog.

There were four big oil furnaces in the barrack. One stood outside my bedroom door. It hummed night and day, but now I noticed with alarm that the hum had ceased. I didn't realize, then, that this was the beginning of a week-long freeze when

Thermometers in Whitehorse registered 70 and 71 degrees below zero (F) on February 3, 1947. Here, the photographer has captured the awesome cold, hanging in the air "like starched gauze," in Whitehorse.

Photo by James Quong.

northwestern Canada and Alaska would know icy depths never experienced before or since.

I was clad in nylon pajamas and my feet were bare as I leaped from my bed onto a small rug. It was like plunging naked into a snowbank. I yanked on flannel-lined ski togs, a heavy sweater, thick socks, fur-trimmed mukluks, parka and mitts. With teeth chattering I ran down the hallway and checked the oil furnaces. They were all cold. I lifted the receiver of the phone and asked the switchboard operator to report Barrack Seventeen frozen solid.

"You're not the only one," she said with a tired sigh. "I've had an avalanche of calls this morning. Stoves are out everywhere. It's sixty-two below in Whitehorse . . . seventy-one at Snag." (Snag, a weather-reporting station off the highway near the Alaska border, was reputed to be the coldest spot in Canada.)

"What about the mess hall?" I gulped.

"It's all right. Steam-heated. Coffee's hot."

Steam heat made me think of the washroom, which was always the warmest room in the barrack. I hurried through the creaky door only to be greeted by the same brittle cold. There was a solid chunk of ice in each of the three toilets. The taps turned without offering a drop of water.

Through the night the furnaces had gone out one by one when the oil in the pipes under the floors had frozen. There weren't any basements in these buildings, and though the pipes were covered with some insulation, they were easy targets for the severe cold.

Outside, a deathly stillness had settled over the world. Not a twig snapped, not a sparrow chirped. Gray smoke trails hung, suspended, above the log cabins and shacks of the town.

Army buses and staff cars did not appear until afternoon. We were informed in the mess hall that stoves were out in the offices in the Dowell area, so dozens of us sat in the Klondyke Cafe slurping coffee and telling stories. That evening I went home to find the barrack in the same state of deep freeze it had been in that morning.

Seven women promptly moved out into the steam-heated Whitehorse Inn. The rest of us went to see a film at one of the local movie houses, which was heated by a wood-burning furnace. When we arrived home, the plumbers were working on the pipes under the floor of the barrack. A banging and clanging of metal on metal, punctuated by the hiss of blowtorches, echoed until morning . . . but the oil remained a stubborn, frozen mass.

Two days later — February 3, 1947 — the pipes in Seventeen were still frozen. On that day the Yukon made headlines around the world. The diary of Northwest Air Command in Edmonton recorded for posterity with a single sentence: "Snag, Yukon set a new record today, 83 degrees below zero. Thermometer will not register any lower." The reading was later changed to 81.4 degrees Fahrenheit when the thermometer was sent to Toronto for recalibration.

Snag air base was located 200 miles northwest of Whitehorse, about sixteen miles off the highway. It was an emergency landing field and an intermediate radio range site — satellite to the RCAF range at Whitehorse. Aircraft flying north were kept on course by contact with these ranges.

A contingent of twenty airmen lived at Snag the year around, and they said that sound travelled with the speed of greased lightning when the mercury hit rock bottom. The howling of huskies at an Indian camp five miles away seemed to put the animals right at their back door. Trees snapped with pistol-like noises that shattered the air. One Yukon wit commented, "At 83 below zero, if given the right wave length, Snag could tune in and hear the angels sing."

G.M. Toole, officer in charge of the Department of Transport's observing station at Snag, said there wasn't any problem with stove oil freezing because the airmen burned wood. However, white gasoline for the use of aircraft turned to slush in the pumps.

One thermometer at the Whitehorse air base read 70 below zero on that historic day. Four more women moved out of Seventeen to seek steam-heated comfort downtown. Rena, Tudy and I were left alone. We asked ourselves if we, too, should move. The steady, unrelenting cold seemed to clout me with bouts of depression. I couldn't make plans for anything exciting. There was always the unconscious struggle to keep warm — a struggle that seemed to blot out all other living. Fear of fire from blowtorches and hot plates was also uppermost in our minds.

Day and night we went from one place that burned wood to the next, in an effort to keep warm. We did not desert Seventeen, however. Perhaps an innate pioneer spirit kept us there. We fell into bed fully clothed, ski togs and all, about midnight each night. We covered ourselves with as many comforters as we could find. Since the electricity was the only utility that was working, we amassed hot plates. In each of our bedrooms, three or four plates were plugged in and glowed red in the middle of our floors. They gave little heat in that awesome ice world, but, like candles, the glow was beautiful and it lasted the night.

My dad had often told me stories about his childhood years growing up on a homestead in Alberta. His family had lived in a tent the first two winters. Gawd! I asked myself if a tent in Alberta could be any worse than a frozen barrack in the Yukon.

* * *

In the Army married quarters on the hill, husbands and wives took turns at thumping outside pipes with sticks to keep the oil stirred up and moving. Blowtorches thawing lines moved around the camp like a battalion of fireflies. Harry Gardiner relaxed his vigil for two hours one night and Jack Frost rewarded him by creeping into his bungalow, stamping out the fire in his furnace, and freezing one of his ears as he lay asleep in bed.

In Dawson City the mercury plunged to 73 below. People sawed cordwood in the bars where they kept warm with belts of over-proof rum. Bartenders paused periodically to shovel the sawdust out of the way so they could get around to wait on customers.

At the repeater station at Watson Lake, one of the airmen realized there was trouble on his line on that memorable day. He could not leave his station, so he phoned thirty-five miles north to the Army bridge-building camp at Little Rancheria River. Sgt.-Maj. Jim Keddell answered the phone. It was 65 degrees below zero. The airman told Keddell that his Varley Loop instrument had indicated interference on the line at Mile 796. Travellers in trouble on the highway in those days often threw a chain over two telephone wires to alert personnel at the nearest repeater station.

Keddell cranked up an Army pickup truck and drove the 126 miles north, where he saw a GMC truck parked at the side of the road. Huddled in the cab were the frozen bodies of three men. The antifreeze had turned to a chunk of ice, and the engine had seized. The gas tank was half full, matches were found in the men's pockets, and there was plenty of scrub spruce near the road. Keddell was sure the men had panicked, because their only effort to survive was a chain, which, a stone's throw away, hung limply over two telephone wires.

The men worked for a gold-mining company in Alaska. They had been on their way to California for a winter vacation.

* * *

The big oil furnace in Blatchford's office was soon perking again. The daytime hours went quickly as there was a lot of work to catch up on.

70

In the evenings, Rena, Tudy and I went to the local theatre in an effort to keep warm. It was good to smell the wood burning in the old furnace in the bowels of the theatre building — but we saw the same movie over again, night after night.

Seventeen defied all manner of effort to thaw pipes. Perfume in bottles froze and a crock of Canadian Club spewed its contents all over a dresser drawer in one of the women's rooms.

On February 8, I was immersed in typing out reports on the condition of motor transport equipment at Fort Nelson when my phone rang. "Hey . . . Seventeen's on fire."

"What?"

"I'm heading that way. You'd better get a drive . . . salvage some clothing." Rena hung up in a hurry.

Blatch drove me home. In front of the barrack ran big hoses, like octopus tentacles, from a fire engine to a fire hydrant on the road. I stepped over these hoses and into the building, where more hoses littered the hallway. There was an acrid smell of stale smoke and charred wood.

"What happened?" I asked one of the firemen.

"A spill of oil around one of the furnaces while it was under attack by a blowtorch sent flames leaping to the ceiling, but . . . everything's OK now."

I thought I smelled the musty aroma of heat. "Hey . . . are the furnaces working?" I asked excitedly.

"See for yourself."

Deep in the belly of each stove, a golden ring of flame flickered. Never before, or since, have I appreciated heat so much.

The water pipes, however, remained frozen. The barrack was at the end of a long line of deserted Army huts, and there was little pressure on the lines. After two weeks of not having any water, several of the women phoned Lt.-Col. J.R.B. Jones, highway engineer, and screamed loudly for some kind of action. Plumbers were out the following day to hook up the water system of the building to the fire hydrant nearby. It was a temporary measure only, and we were told that in the spring Seventeen would be closed and we would have to find other living quarters.

Chapter 13

A marching band thumped down the main street of Whitehorse. In a fenced-off enclosure on the sidewalk, the bearded judge of a kangaroo court banged his gavel on a table top and hollered at the dejected-looking soldier: "Guilty . . . guilty. Fined three dollars for not growing a beard."

Across the street, a sign in front of a barber shop proclaimed, in bold letters: YOU GROW 'EM — WE'LL DYE 'EM.

Carnival time. I loved every second of it . . . dog sleds on the river . . . ski competitions . . . hockey games . . . races over the White Pass with contestants carrying 100 pounds strapped to their backs in memory of the pioneers of 1898. Diamond Tooth Gerties and Lime Juice Lils shook their bustled rumps at men in a Mardi Gras, dance-hall atmosphere in one of the Air Force hangars. Life was filled once more with wonder, enchantment.

Tim walked out of the crowd at the big final bash that brought the four-day carnival to a close. Music and laughter echoed to the rafters of the cavernous hangar.

"Jeez . . . this place is crowded, kid. How can you stand the pushing and the noise?" he asked.

"I love it . . . can rub shoulders with the greats of Yukon history . . . George Carmack, Skookum Jim, Tagish Charlie."

"Kee-rist . . . they even look like them," he said, laughing, as clones of Carmack, Jim and Charlie walked past, giving me a mock bow. Historically, all three had been responsible (along with the controversial Bob Henderson) for discovering gold in 1897 near Dawson City. By 1947, Dawson's population had dwindled to about 200 residents. This was a far cry from the gold rush days, when the town was bursting at the seams with 10,000 people scrambling after a fortune. Dawson was 400 miles downriver — northwest of Whitehorse. It had been seat of the territorial government since 1898, when the Yukon had been created a separate territory by act of Parliament (The Yukon Act) and provision had been made for a local government composed of a chief executive-style commissioner and a legislative council.

Winter carnival days in February brought the excitement of kangaroo courts, dancing, races on foot over the White Pass, and dog races on the river. Here, a dog team is shown resting.

Photo by James Quong.

In 1942, when American Army engineers built the Alaska Highway, they bypassed Dawson by 335 miles. Whitehorse then had a greater advantage with its swelling population, a big, busy airfield, and a road that linked it with the outside world. By 1946, the cry to transfer government offices from Dawson to the southern location became loud and strong. The transfer did not occur, however, until 1950, when a mayor and council were elected to govern the new city of Whitehorse.

* * *

The dance-hall girls did a final cancan. Gertie's diamond tooth sparkled like a real, giant rock each time she smiled. In keeping with tradition, the men threw coins onto the stage, and, as the last curtain came down on my first Yukon carnival, Tim and I slipped out into a starry, cold night and headed downtown for the beer parlor at the Whitehorse Inn. Tim had told me the Inn had changed hands three times in a decade, in a toss of dice at the Ace Away game. T.C. Richards, a big man who often wore a ten-gallon Stetson, was the current owner. He had been the last to win the famous hotel, for a $3,000 gamble and a lucky toss of the dice.

The small beverage room was too noisy, too bright, and it reeked of draft beer. We managed to get a table in a corner where the noise was somewhat muted.

"I've spent a month at an Eskimo village about one hundred miles this side of Aklavik. Gawd . . . it's good to see the bright lights again," Tim said.

"A month? That's a long time for you to stay in one place?"

"Yeah . . . well . . . was forced t' stay there. Had a stroke of bad luck."

"Bad luck?" The palms of my hands went clammy.

"Hit a downdraft when I was comin' in for a landing. Jeez . . . that old aircraft must've fallen five hundred feet. Boom. When we stopped, it was like hitting cement. The whole damn load shifted . . . and I had a big load . . . lumber, tents, clothing, food. Lucky I had altitude. But, unknown to me, one ski had been knocked loose."

"Loose?"

"Yeah . . . like dangling, at a ninety-degree angle."

"To the ground?"

He nodded. "And you didn't know about it?"

He shook his head. "No. There isn't any radio communication in the village . . . nothing but a bunch of quonset huts, and, on

74

that day, a crowd of people looking up."

"And they couldn't let you know about the ski?"

"Not unless they spelled out something in the snow, but, I was comin' in for a landing, so there wasn't time. I came in as if I had two good skis. Gawd . . . when I hit ground, I did everything but turn a somersault."

"Really?"

"Yeah. Spun in circles, lurched —" He paused, shook his head sadly. "Damn. I thought my number was up."

"You weren't hurt?"

"Not a scratch. My mechanic, too . . . okay. It was just the plane, the undercarriage and the skis. Kaput."

"What did you do?"

"Well . . . they flew me in two more skis from Edmonton, and my mechanic and two Eskimos and I worked on that damn plane until we had it back in shape."

"And now?"

"Now, I'm stuck here while it goes through a safety check."

I sighed. "Life's fragile."

"You wanna believe."

"Does your mother know about these . . . these close calls?" I gulped.

"Maw? No . . . but, in her own quiet way, she's aware . . . I mean she knows . . . that I live a dangerous life." He paused a moment in thought. "You'd like my mother. She'd never try to stop me from doing what I want to do. She often used to say, 'And sure, Tim, I don't much care what you do in life, whether you're a shoemaker or prime-minister of Canada. You just be the *best* shoemaker, or the *best* prime-minister'. "

He was the oldest of five children who were active in hockey, basketball and drama in their hometown, Kirkland Lake, Ontario. His father worked in a gold mine at Kirkland. They were Irish Catholics who attended Mass regularly, but Tim had left the fold, never going to church anymore. And yet, in spite of this, he was a spiritual person.

"I can see God in nature," he once said. "When you look at the sun setting across this vast, unpeopled rim of the world, you get a gut feeling that a Creator is out there, somewhere."

As we sat in the beer parlor at the inn, I felt nervous thinking about how close he'd come to being killed, and I was relieved when somebody struck a chord on an old piano. We sang a hearty rendition of the song "I'll Be With You When The Ice Worms Nest Again," then the pianist led the boisterous crowd into nostalgia with "There's A Long, Long Trail A-Winding." After this, Tim said, "Let's go slumming . . . over to the 98 Ballroom where there's a Wurlitzer that's usually jumping."

Tim was dressed in a turtleneck sweater and dark brown corded pants instead of the trim pilot's uniform. He seemed more relaxed than I'd ever seen him. We dumped our parkas on a bench at the 98, and danced in our flight boots. The wooden floor rose and fell with the pounding of hobnailed boots, winter footwear and moccasins, and we laughed till the tears came.

The 98 was a rough place where drunks and prostitutes hung out. Indians berserk on home-brew often drew knives, but they were not as dangerous as soldiers from remote highway camps who came to town for excitement and poured into the 98 to start brawls. Many of the young men from No. 1 Road had quite a reputation for brawling.

On this particular night, a fight broke out. Knives flashed. When we saw the RCMP officers coming in the front door, Tim and I ducked out the back way. It was 2 a.m.

He stopped in front of Seventeen, enfolded me in his arms and kissed me 'til my toes tingled.

"I love you, love you, love you," he whispered. "Let's go to the inn . . . spend a couple o' nights, together."

A little voice within me cried, "Go . . . go. You love him. Seize the day." And another voice warned, "Don't be foolish. You might get pregnant, and then what?"

"No," I whispered, uncertainly, still struggling with those warring tides of feeling.

"Why?"

"Because . . . there'll always be the other woman."

The following day I saw him briefly at the airport where I went to pick up a parcel Dad had sent to me. He was on his way to talk to the guys in the control tower.

"My plane's okay. I'm leaving today for Old Crow . . . but look, let's do that again. Go dancing, drinking."

"Sure. Call me when you hit town again."

We parted. The terminal where Ralph had left the parcel was full of people waiting to board a Dak that had just come in from Fairbanks. As I turned to leave, a wan face in the crowd triggered a memory. I paused, looked again.

"Anne? Anne Peterson?"

She reached out with one arm as though greeting a lost friend. "Oh, Hope . . . it's . . . it's good to see you again."

"You had your baby?" I asked, seeing the bundle of blankets curled up in her arm.

"A girl. Two months old," she said proudly.

There was a small suitcase at her feet. "You're going out for a vacation?"

She shook her head sadly. "For good. Ian and I . . . well . . . we've decided to part. I . . . he likes it here, but I don't. We almost froze to death in that awful cold. Our furnace kept going out. It was —" Her voice broke. "You can have this country."

I wished her well and left, but a line from Robert Service kept rolling around in my head: "This is the law of the Yukon, that only the strong shall survive."

I wondered then about the survivors. Were we strong, or foolish? In spite of having to work alone, often, in the office, in spite of the trauma of the killing cold . . . I was beginning to like this country north of the 60th parallel.

Chapter 14

In mid-March came a deluge of warm rain. It was like a Chinook — melting the snow, giving us a brief taste of spring. This interlude in winter seemed to be a good time for Reemee and Service Corps to evaluate the effect of the severe cold of February on equipment and men. Major Blatchford and Major Nicholson put their findings on this subject on paper, and I was busy typing out the reports one rainy afternoon.

To remedy the freezing of gas lines in staff cars and diesel-operated equipment, Blatchford and Nicholson found that adding one quart of alcohol to twelve gallons of gasoline, and one quart of alcohol to twenty-five gallons of diesel fuel, was a must. The alcohol was added to the bulk fuel in the pumps.

Synthetic brake hoses on the cars froze and crystallized at 20 below zero, and on application of pressure on the brake linings, the hoses burst. The brake hose problem was not rectified until two years later, when the Army approved new brake hoses that were able to withstand rock-bottom temperatures.

A winter operations report said, in part: "The weather was a great trial to the soldier who worked constantly outside. Morale, generally measured in the ability of a man to do a job, was very low. To offset these effects, it was necessary to operate essential services only, and to rest the men as much as possible."

As I typed out these and other reports that Major Blatchford had dictated to me, the rain beat against the windows of the office. I was alone, and my mind often wandered to The Valley. I hadn't heard from Brad since New Year's Eve. I wondered if he was still eager to go into The Valley. Should I contact him, or would he contact me?

The phone rang to interrupt my work and musings. Brigadier Walsh's deep voice rang across the wires. He wanted to talk to Major Blatchford. I told him that Blatchford had gone to MacRae early that morning. An hour later Walsh paid me a visit in the office. He was a tall, good-looking man with dark hair and a dark moustache. He was always accompanied by Major Sarantos, who,

78

Brigadier Walsh pinpoints a location as his aide looks on, at Whitehorse in August of 1946. He served nearly two years as the commander of the Northwest Highway System.
Photo by J. Long, courtesy Public Archives Canada

as D.A.A. & Q.M.G., was chief administrative staff officer to Walsh. A friendly person with a warm smile, Sarantos, leash in hand, toted Walsh's dog — an English cocker spaniel the brigadier called "a perfect gun dog."

Walsh was thirty-eight at that time, every inch a soldier in his khaki uniform, with erect carriage and bold blue eyes. He had been twice mentioned in dispatches during the war for exceptional work beyond the line of duty. Lt.-Col. J.R.B. Jones (who later became a brigadier and served as commander of the NWHS from 1957 to 1960), in a talk to graduate engineers in

A snowy section of the northern highway, with an S-curve, runs near Christmas Creek Summit, Mile 1047.9. Mountains of the St. Elias Range loom in the background.
Photo by James Quong.

Edmonton in 1948, paid a tribute to Walsh as follows:

A group of officers and ordinary ranks (of the Canadian Army) arrived in Whitehorse in January and February, 1946. We took over a strange unknown ribbon of road covered with snow. We knew the vehicles and equipment left us (from the U.S. Army) were old and worn and needed immediate replacement. We had no married quarters, and I, like most of the Army up there, had been home only a few months after five or six years of separation. It looked grim. We read the records of how the rivers rose suddenly in the spring and took out dozens of bridges; we were told of flash floods that sprang from mountain slopes to wash out miles of highway. It looked grimmer. We took another look at the old and decrepit road machinery, the tremendous task of sorting out warehouses full of unlisted tools and spare parts, and the way our proposed establishment had been pared down. It looked hopeless. However, with the drive of Brigadier Walsh, we got cracking.

It was this man — Brigadier Walsh, who exuded much energy and charisma — confronting me on that rainy afternoon in March, 1947. He said he had driven the ten miles to MacRae and Major Blatchford was not there. He said it matter-of-factly, not accusingly. However, I hadn't heard from the major, so I couldn't suggest where to look for him. After hearing this, Walsh walked around the large office divided in the middle by filing cabinets. He seemed preoccupied, thoughtful. Then, abruptly, he turned and left.

I had only seen Walsh in the distance until that day. Many people seemed to be in awe of him, but I wished he had sat down and told me about his career. I was particularly interested in what had brought him to the wild Northwest. Perhaps this urge to look more deeply into the life of this first commander of the NWHS was simply the journalist in me coming out. I knew, even then, that his service record had been impressive. He went overseas in May, 1940, and served in Sicily, Spitzbergen, and elsewhere in Italy and northwestern Europe. He commanded 1 and 4 Divisions, and later was chief engineer for the Canadian Army. He organized the takeover of the Alaska Highway for the Canadian Army and would spend nearly two years as commander NWHS, directing operations at a time when money and enthusiasm for keeping the Alaska Highway open were at a low ebb.

* * *

That day I came home after work to find Brad waiting for me. The warm rain must have made him think of The Valley, too. He told me he'd rented a Waco, and that he'd be leaving Whitehorse on July 1, stopping briefly at Fort Nelson. The next day he'd go on into The Valley.

"I'm taking an Indian guide with me — Jimmy Pete. He knows that country where the bombers went down . . . knows it like the back of his hand. It's rough land . . . mountains, sheer cliffs."

"I'm not afraid," I said bravely, in spite of a few nagging worries about a small plane and a valley so remote it was like a pinpoint in outer space. "What do I need to take with me? Bed roll, parka, grub?"

"Bed roll, parka, knee-high caulk boots for hiking, warm ski pants. No grub. I have this and everything else under control. We'll be gone about five days."

Marg Moses, a slim dark-haired friend of mine from another barrack, came in to see me. "Hi. You two look like conspirators," she said. Then, after taking off her coat and dumping it over a chair, she joined us.

"You still working for the Army, Marg?" Brad asked.

"Right. And you? Still making jewelry of scrap metal from that ghost valley?"

"Sure, but you'll have t' come over and see my ranch."

"In Whiskey Flats?"

"Yeah. The district isn't much, but I've got a nice place."

"I heard you'd gone back to flying."

"Not me. Never."

He lit a cigarette. "I'm going into Million Dollar Valley again in July . . ." He paused, and I jumped in to finish the sentence.

"And I'm going with him."

Marg's gray eyes widened. "That's quite an adventure."

On that note I went into my room and took a bottle of wine out of my dresser drawer. We made sandwiches and dug up a candle for the table. We ate, drank and shared stories about the Yukon. Brad grew quiet, often not hearing us when we spoke to him. He seemed absorbed in another world, or perhaps, I thought, he had a lot on his mind with regard to the flight into The Valley. Finally I could stand his brooding no longer. I slapped him on the back and said jovially, "Hey . . . wake up."

He leaped to his feet, turned and shook a warning finger at me. "Don't you ever do that again, young lady. I . . . I'm nervous as hell. Any guy who's been in a sky war comes out pretty jumpy."

He lit a cigarette with trembling fingers.

"Sorry," I said, not knowing what else to say.

He took several quick drags on his cigarette. "Look . . . why don't you girls come over t' my place. I think we could all stand a stiff drink . . . not that the wine didn't hit the spot."

He had purchased a War Assets jeep that he drove like a fighter plane, and we were glad to get out of it at his door. On entering his house, I was shocked at the disarray. The wooden shelves had been pulled down from the walls and piled in the middle of the floor. Wall plaques, bookends, crosses, knickknacks were strewn across the heavy glass top of the display case which was unplugged and dark inside. A bare yellow bulb, dangling from a cord in the ceiling, threw a dingy glow around the room.

In the kitchen, the sink was overflowing with dishes. The place seemed cold, and he put spruce logs into the kitchen range, stoked the fire, and brewed a pot of strong coffee to which he added a healthy splash of rum. He poured three mugs of coffee. Nobody spoke. It seemed right to be silent. It wasn't a brooding quiet, just a lull in conversation until Brad settled down and joined us. But . . . he didn't settle down. He paced restlessly back and forth across the kitchen, drinking coffee and rum from a thick white mug that had a big yellow stain on one side.

"You know . . . sometimes I get so bloody bored in this place . . ." He motioned irritably to the four walls. "I . . . I just can't figure out what gets into me. I've made a fortune with this jewelry business, and . . . well . . . still I'm fed up."

He put his coffee mug down on the table. "Look . . . don't get scared. I'm . . . I'm just gonna liven things up."

He opened a drawer in the table, and took out a handgun.

"German Luger," he said, pointing the barrel at the far wall. "My buddy picked it up on a battlefield in France."

I tensed. He backed up to give himself distance. Thoughts tumbled through my head in wild confusion. What was he going to do? I was poised, ready to run out. And yet, I had a lot of respect for Tim Condon. A friend of Tim's wouldn't be a crazy fool. I tried to remain calm, seated on a bench against the table, staring at this man who seemed mad. Marg's eyes blinked nervously. Clinging to her seat at the table, she too watched in worried wonder. He squinted down the barrel of the gun, turned it, and pulled the trigger again and again. The noise was like firecrackers exploding. The room filled with the acrid smell of gunpowder. I sat frozen. He laughed like a hyena in heat.

"Look at them go . . . look . . . look at those goddam knotholes flying."

More wild laughter, more shooting, then a pause.

Nobody spoke. Tension hung in the air like the prelude to an earthquake. More fragmented laughter. More flying bullets. More knotholes popping out of the wooden walls with deadly accuracy. Another pause. His khaki-colored cotton shirt was wet with perspiration. He leaned against the wall, his arms falling limply at his sides. Everything about him sagged. The silence was super-charged with emotion, ready to burst at any second. We waited. We stared. We thought of slinking out like Indians sliding into the sunset. Nobody moved. Then . . . Brad straightened up, walked calmly over to the kitchen table, opened the drawer, tenderly put the gun away, closed the drawer, sat down on a rough bench near the table, lit a cigarette, blew smoke rings and talked to the rings.

"It's hell to come out of combat and have to settle down. It's like that other you is still over there, somewhere."

Silence.

After a few seconds, I stood and put my coat on. "Look . . . Brad . . . we have to go, but we'll walk. I feel like exercise."

"Me, too," said Marg, rising quickly and trying to struggle into her parka.

"No," said Brad emphatically. "I'll take you home."

As we got out of the jeep at the door of Seventeen, he called out, "I'll be in touch."

Marg and I sat drinking tea in my room for an hour.

"He's really weird, isn't he?" said Marg.

"A screw loose? Missed too many boats?"

After a few moments of thought, Marg shook her head.

"You don't think he's missed too many boats?"

"No. I have this deep, gut feeling that he's a gentle, sensitive soul, but he's like a lot of guys up here . . . trying desperately to find the right bridge from that science fiction world of yesterday to the real world of today."

She echoed my thoughts.

* * *

March went out like a lamb, and on Queen Victoria's birthday in May the Yukon was the hottest spot in Canada. I climbed straight up from the valley floor near the barrack to the top of the Air Force Hill. The early afternoon sun was hot on my shoulders; it threatened to burn my bare arms. The town, nestled in a cradle of mountains, was a shimmering haze of heat. It was 85 above zero. The ice-bound world of winter was long behind me. I felt like a sourdough as I contemplated a new adventure into a valley of ghost bombers.

Chapter 15

In June, Dad sent me five $100 Canadian bonds he had purchased for me during the war. In the letter that accompanied the bonds he gave me a colorful picture of the new oil age in Alberta.

"As you know, Leduc Number One blew in with a roar on February 13 in a farmer's field seventeen miles south of Edmonton. The city was beginning to recover from the invasion of U.S. troops to build the Alaska Highway, and then . . . the oil era hit. We're overrun by men in gum boots and hard hats. They're drilling deep into the earth around Leduc, Woodbend and Redwater. Old Bible Bill Aberhart promised every man, woman and child twenty-five dollars a month if we elected his Social Credit party to power in 1935. We did, but he never gave us anything except a fire-and-brimstone sermon on radio every Sunday morning. Now, however, we may see that twenty-five dollars in oil royalties — maybe!"

I sighed, thinking of the new excitement at home . . . and a busy newsroom at the *Edmonton Bulletin* where I'd worked for many happy hours, and where I'd held philosophical talks with city editor John Oliver. I had not forgotten my pen. Late at night I often sat in bed, propped up by pillows, writing notes or stray lines of poetry. My big story was coming up, though . . . The Valley. Sometimes, macabre shapes of planes floated through my dreams.

Once I'd mentioned The Valley to a hard-nosed Scottish sergeant in the Royal Canadian Mounted Police force. He'd shrugged indifferently as he pointed to a poster he had just finished tacking to a light pole near the headquarters building.

"Och . . . there're four hundred planes missing in this Yukon . . . four hundred we'll bloody-well never find. Read that."

I studied the handsome face on the poster, the face of a young lieutenant in the uniform of the U.S. Army Air Force. A warm rain swirled around me like an Irish mist, and it washed over the nearly life-sized face of the airman. The dark, melancholy eyes seemed to be crying real tears as the mist condensed and rolled down the cheeks. The picture seemed so real that I shivered as I read the bold print at the bottom: "A thousand dollars will be paid to anyone knowing the whereabouts of Lieut. William Andrew Dodds who disappeared June 30, 1942, while flying a P-40 from Los Angeles to Ladd Field."

I thought of the miles and miles of hairbrush forests where a mortal could disappear . . . a star, shooting into a bottomless sea.

* * *

Apart from thinking about my trip into The Valley, I was involved in trying to keep Radio Station CFWH on the air. The Armed Forces Radio Broadcasts in Los Angeles had cut White-horse out of the northern circuit because all of the U.S. troops had left the area. Mac was worried. It was difficult to fill all operating hours with live talent. He phoned Los Angeles, and he was told that if we could locate even one U.S. serviceman in Whitehorse, the AFRB would be reinstated. We began our search for that one member of the U.S. Armed Forces.

In the meantime, I was able to get the Rev. Harold Lee, a Baptist minister, to sing for half an hour, accompanied on the studio organ by his wife. Mona MacDonald, wife of Sgt. Hector MacDonald of No. 1 Road, offered to play jazz piano numbers for half an hour, and a civilian cook from the mess hall volunteered to play the piano and sing a medley of tunes. The cook became a problem because he arrived quite drunk, every night. A local storyteller filled the cook's spot with yarns of the North. The news and happenings took fifteen minutes, and I read a roundup of local news and happenings for another fifteen minutes. This left me with four hours to fill in with music, from records which still sat in heaps on the floor.

In a month we located a U.S. Armed Forces flier who flew from Fairbanks to Whitehorse on a regular, weekly basis. We were put back on circuit for the Armed Forces Radio Broadcasts. Mac and his gang breathed a great sigh of relief.

Chapter 16

Paul was a young private with the NWHS who was stationed in Whitehorse. He often came over to Seventeen to use the big treadle sewing machine that had been left to us — a legacy from the U.S. Army.

Paul was born in Halifax, Nova Scotia, grew up there, enlisted in the Army in 1942, and went overseas for three years. He received an honorable discharge from the Army in 1945, re-enlisted in '46 and was sent to Whitehorse.

His mother had taught him to do invisible mending and he used the sewing machine for this type of repair work on his uniforms, shirts, parkas, sweatshirts, and even his sweaters. At odd times, he mended clothes for those friends who couldn't sew. He was proud of his sewing skills, was not inhibited by people, had a good sense of humor and would never take a penny for any repair work he did for us. We loved to have him join us for coffee and doughnuts after his mending sprees.

One evening I was busy ironing while Paul was sewing. We talked, but he seemed a little depressed. He wasn't the kind of person to keep his emotions bottled up, and finally he told me that he was in love with a young Indian woman who lived in Whitehorse and who had received her education at the Roman Catholic convent there.

"Last week I asked my C.O. for permission to marry Dyea, and . . . he got angry. Wow! Told me a definite 'no,' said that if I went ahead and got married I'd get my walking ticket."

In those days a private in the Canadian Army had to have the consent of his commanding officer to marry. If the C.O. felt the soldier was setting himself up for a stormy relationship by contemplating a marriage that would mix races or religions or whatever, then he could withhold consent. We were feeling our way back into a peacetime world back then, and many young soldiers were questioning this Big Brother influence in their lives.

I'd heard rumors that Paul was a "squaw man." I hated the label. It painted a picture of a hard-drinking, hard-fisted male and a submissive, shy, uneducated woman who was often beaten, impregnated and left to the mercy of the next itinerant worker.

Paul was not a traditional "squaw man." He spoke of Dyea gently, with a lot of respect. He took an odd drink in the men's canteen, but he was not a drunk. He felt at ease with women, was genuinely fond of them, and yet he was popular with men, too. He played a tough game of baseball in the summer and basketball in the winter.

I often saw Paul and Dyea at the local movie theatre, where the division between Indians and whites was as blatant as the crudest color line. The whole front of the theatre (divided by a walkway) was called "Indian Heaven." Whites did not sit in Indian Heaven if they wanted to maintain their good reputations. And . . . Indians did not cross the line to sit in the white section for fear of being ridiculed or physically tossed out.

I often saw Paul seated beside Dyea in Indian Heaven. And sometimes I saw a friend of Paul's . . . Larry, also a private in the Army . . . seated with Dyea's sister. Both young women were attractive, well-dressed, well-spoken in English as well as in their own Native Athapascan Indian tongue.

One weekend there was a double wedding at the Roman Catholic church, and a month later I saw a goodbye ceremony outside the Reemee office. It had all the points of drama surrounding the Alfred Dreyfus tragedy in France in 1894. The crimes were not the same, however. Dreyfus was falsely accused of spy activities by the French Army; Paul and Larry had married women of whom the Canadian Army did not approve. The movie of the Dreyfus case showed the drums rolling and half the French Army assembled in a parade square. For two Canadian Army privates on that June day in 1947 in Whitehorse, Yukon Territory, there was no fanfare.

I could not hear what the company sergeant-major was saying outside the building to the two "delinquents." The windows were closed and he had his back to me as I tried to look through the glass, from inside our office, without being seen.

The early afternoon was cool. A wishy-washy sun was struggling to shine through low-hanging clouds. The men were wearing fatigues with no insignia. I recalled again the movie and the high-ranking officer who reached out and tore the insignia of rank from Captain Dreyfus's tunic. Paul and Larry, facing the C.S.M., would be spared this humiliation.

They were presented with an envelope each. I could only guess what was in the envelope. Discharge papers? Honorable? Dishonorable? Final pay?

They stood to attention, then finally at ease as cordial good-byes were said. The following winter I saw them selling cordwood door-to-door, trying to make a living.

* * *

Brad phoned me on a Saturday morning following this goodbye ceremony. "How would you like to go to Otter Falls for the afternoon?" he said.

I was glad of the invitation to get out of Whitehorse for a few hours. I needed the respite. What I didn't know was that the sun would fall out of the sky for me before the day was over.

The falls was located fifty miles north, a few miles off the highway. It was a gorgeous location with mountains and cascading water. We climbed to the top of a high hill. It was an exhilarating climb. There were patches of snow here and there at the top. We sat on a granite rock and looked down into a mountain lake that seemed like a pond, it was so far away. Hoary old peaks were mirrored in the crystal-clear water. The sun on our shoulders was warm, penetrating.

"I had to get away from civilization," Brad said, out of breath from the climb. He paused, lit a cigarette with trembling fingers, took a long drag, blew out the smoke. "I have to talk to you."

"Shoot."

"I . . . I'm not going into The Valley. I . . . I have to cancel."

"What?" I cried, astounded. I'd already purchased nearly half the gear I needed.

"I'm going back to flying."

"Where?"

"The Middle East."

"Israel?"

"Maybe."

"A soldier of fortune?"

"Perhaps." He looked me full in the face. The sky-blue eyes were intense. "It's what I want. I've tried to conform . . . tried to do what my mother, father, wife . . . yes, dammit, I've got a wife and two children living in Winnipeg . . . what they all wanted me to do. Come down from that high of the war, settle in on civvy street. I've tried. It didn't work."

He took another quick drag from his cigarette. "The chance to go back to flying came suddenly, two days ago."

Somewhere deep inside of me a raw nerve twitched. I couldn't speak. I understood his motive, his need, but the disappointment within me was overwhelming until I felt a stern resolve build up.

I would go into The Valley. Not tomorrow, nor the next day, nor the next, but . . . someday. It was meant to be. I felt a strong new destiny unfolding. I would go into The Valley. Alone.

He broke the silence in a gentle voice. "There's another reason why I'm going back to flying. I . . . I don't know how to say this, Hope. I've even thought of not saying it."

A chill zigzagged up my backbone. I reached for my sweater, which I'd dropped on the rock beside me. He helped me into it, then sat limply, looking at his hands, the long fingers intertwined in front of him.

"What's wrong?" I said. "What?"

He cleared his throat, stroked his blond beard. "Tim Condon was killed last week."

"Tim?" I choked. "You don't mean it?" I stood up, feeling dizzy. He stood, put a warm arm around me. "You're lying. I'd have heard. On the news."

He shook his head. "Nobody cares about a lone airman beyond the reaches of civilization."

I felt empty. "It's true, actually true?"

He nodded, his face screwed up in pain. "I wish it wasn't."

"Where?"

"Old Crow. He was flying in fog, hit an air pocket, never recovered."

I couldn't ask the next question, and he seemed to sense it.

"There'll be a quiet, family funeral. In Kirkland Lake."

He turned, lifted his Luger from a holster under his plaid wool jacket, aimed the gun at the lake in the distance, emptied the barrel into the water.

"Life's short. I'm gonna live every goddam minute the way I want to," he shouted. Then, quietly, he put the gun away.

We climbed down from the mountain.

Chapter 17

I put Tim out of my mind and stoically went about my everyday business. A robot could not have performed better. Then one night I reached for a book from my small bookcase. *Lord Jim* by Conrad — a book Tim had given me — fell into my hands. Inside the front cover was a brief note, "I hope you enjoy this story as much as I did."

A tidal wave of anger rose within me at sight of his handwritten message. Tears spurted out. I threw myself on the bed, banged the pillows with my fists. Although The Valley of Lost Planes had really brought us together, our relationship had developed beyond that one interest. There had been an abundance of unconditional affection and respect on both sides. I screamed out a whole barrage of whys: Why had he died? Why had I not gone to bed with him when we both wanted it so much? I revelled in self- pity and cried myself to sleep.

The next day I felt exhausted, but I knew I could not fold up and die. Tim would want me to go on . . . to let life flow around me, to enjoy my friends and, finally, to carry a torch into The Valley. A strong determination rose within me. I would go into The Valley. I would go.

I did not mention the tragedy to Tudy, Rena or Betty. Tudy alone had briefly met Tim. We women who worked for the Army seldom met Air Force people. The RCAF camp was a self-sufficient unit, located on top of the hill; the Army NWHS camp was also self-contained, situated between the Air Force and the town of Whitehorse. The taxi man, Sam, had been right on that bleak morning of my arrival. Communication between these three small towns was minimal, although a Board of Trade in Whitehorse helped maintain dialogue at an uppper-echelon level.

Not until March 6, 1950, did the people of Whitehorse vote in favor of municipal government. The "town" was then declared a city. Until that time, however, it was a scattering of people, many of them squatters. Before the U.S. Army descended on the town in 1942, there were 500 residents. The population swelled to 30,000 during the war years — 1942 to 1945. In the late 40s, however, Army, Air Force and town combined numbered close to 5,000 people.

I did not see Brad again. His cabin in Whiskey Flats was quickly filled with itinerants who worked on an Army road gang. I'd made up my mind, though, to pursue The Valley . . . to seek it alone. Each day I renewed my vow to go . . . in memory of Tim.

The Army notified those of us in Seventeen that the barrack would be closed the end of June, and we were to relocate in one of the other two women's barracks. Or . . . we could move into quarters downtown. There were always small houses for rent, usually three rooms for $50 a month — buy and split your own wood, pay for your own electricity and telephone, haul your own water from the river. A few hardy types rented downtown cabins. I was fortunate to find a room in Barrack Forty-seven. Directly across the hall, Betty settled in, and on either side of Betty, Tudy and Rena. I was happy to be surrounded by friends. I needed these friends. They were lively. They helped me forget Tim.

We often hollered at one another from room to room. The walls did not join the peaked roof. The area was left open above door-ways along the length of the hall (as it had been in Seventeen) so heat from furnaces would circulate.

We moved on a Saturday morning. Two Reemee soldiers received permission from Blatchford to use an Army pickup truck to help us move. We hauled books, clothes, trunks, lamps, rugs, booze . . . everything that wasn't built-in. At five o'clock, just when I thought I had all under control in my new room, the curtain rod fell down, drapes and all. I borrowed a hammer and was busy walloping a nail into place in the window frame, when a short, rather frail young woman came into my room.

"Stop that . . . stop that noise," she whispered, covering her ears.

I had seen her at odd times around the camp. She'd always kept to herself. I was told that she worked as a clerk for one of the Army offices in the Dowell area. I looked down at her from my perch on a chair.

"My room's the one next door, and . . . and really . . . I've never known such noise until . . . until you people moved in."

"You're Agnes, aren't you?" I asked gently.

She nodded. "And you're Hope?"

Before I had a chance to say "yes" she plunged on quickly, never raising her voice above a whisper. "Do you realize that God is peace and love, and there's not much peace and love around here?"

She studied me in a sly way, watching what the impact of the words would do. I was so surprised I just stared. Then I noticed that she wore a floor-length nightgown and bathrobe. A wool tam was pulled down on her forehead, and I remembered that somebody had once said she wore the tam all the time.

"It's only five o'clock. I . . . I . . . you're ready for bed, Agnes? I mean . . . it's so early."

"I go to bed every night at five o'clock. I go to bed to pray for sinners."

"Oh?"

"Sinners stay up till all hours of the night."

"Oh?"

Again that sly look.

"Agnes . . . I'll try to be quieter. Sorry. I'm sure you couldn't sleep with all that banging."

"I'll pray for you. You need prayers." She frowned accusingly, turned and left.

I sat on the side of the bed, hammer still in hand. While I wondered what to do about this strange apparition who lived next door, my friends tiptoed into my room, and, convulsing with laughter, sat on the floor.

"What's the matter with you guys? You crazy?" I asked.

More stifled laughter, until their humor rubbed off on me and I saw the whole scene with Agnes as a comedy. She couldn't be real, I thought. We laughed, choking back the noise until tears spilled over. When we couldn't contain our outbursts anymore, we tiptoed down the hall into the reception room where we closed the door. Here it was more contained. No open spaces. We collapsed into Chesterfields and easy chairs.

"How can we be quiet? It's not our nature. And . . . quiet from five o'clock, every night? Jesus. She's nuts," Betty howled.

"Agnes used to work for the Americans. She's always been weird," Tudy said.

"Well . . . I don't care what you guys say. I wish she wouldn't pick on me," I said.

More wild laughter. "You're a sinner, Hope. Why shouldn't she pick on you?"

"Oh, shut up," I howled.

* * *

One night I came home after work and turned on my radio. Sometimes, if we were lucky, we were able to pick up Vancouver on shortwave. Dad had sent me a powerful little radio set, and on this particular night I tuned in to a jazz concert. Ever mindful of Agnes, I turned the volume low . . . as low as I could and still hear it. Soon there was a banging on the wall. When I didn't pay any attention, a pale ghost of a woman in blue night attire and a brown wool tam tiptoed in.

"I just can't sleep, Hope . . . and that jazz is sin . . . black, blatant sin. Do you want to go to hell?"

The whispering voice was strange. I always found myself whispering back and wondering why. Since I didn't want to get into an argument with Agnes, I shut off the set and went to a movie with Rena. Later that night, as we buttered crackers with cheese for a bedtime snack in the reception room, we were confronted again by our neighbor.

"Do you have to talk so loud . . . laugh so loud . . . stay out so late?"

In the days that followed, we found ourselves tiptoeing around the barrack, whispering to one another, trying to perform tasks without any noise. One evening, when Betty was changing a light bulb in her lamp, she dropped the bulb on the bare floor. The noise shattered the quiet like the shot from a revolver.

"What are you doing?" came the voice in a strange, loud wail.

We began to long for the camaraderie that had existed in old Seventeen.

One morning Agnes had showered in the big bathroom located the width of the building at the opposite end from the reception room. She emerged from the shower draped in towels. Most of the young women ran around in the nude in the bathroom, or certainly half-dressed. I'd had a shower that morning, and was seated on a bench drying myself. Agnes studied me in a distasteful way, raking me over from head to foot with her large blue eyes.

"The nude body is sinful. Cover it," she demanded in a husky whisper, turning away with aversion. I picked up my bathrobe and put it on.

"What's sinful about the human body?" I asked, feeling exasperated.

"The wages of sin are death."

I stared at her. As she stood in front of me, her hair damp, her body swathed in a big brown bath towel, I thought she was rather attractive. The infernal tam had been discarded for the shower, and she looked rather fragile, her eyes large and luminous in a pale, oval face. There was a saucy spattering of freckles across her nose. I towered above her. She looked up at me with a certain defiance.

"The wages of sin are death, and don't you ever forget it."

94

"Look, Agnes . . . get lost. You and I don't talk the same language." I picked up my towel and left.

* * *

Several weeks later, when I was having a late supper in the mess hall, I heard fire engines screaming in the distance. Fire was uppermost in our minds at all times. The Army and Air Force buildings were built from spruce lumber that was now dry. In the town, many shacks and shanties had been hastily erected as close together as ants in a hill.

As the fire sirens screamed, those of us still eating wondered where the fire was located until a civilian employee came running in and announced, "The Reemee shop is burning."

I ran the half-mile to the shop, where flames roared skyward. Black smoke belched out from the roof. I could see heavy equipment and Army vehicles inside the building; they were sketched boldly against the flames, like skeletons, where one wall had caved in.

The crowd that had gathered was held 500 feet away from the fire by firemen. Hoses crisscrossed the ground. I saw Mac stepping over the debris, his tall, angular figure outlined against the flames. In Army fatigues and heavy boots that were covered with mud, he looked like a battle-weary soldier as he nervously paced around the burning structure.

With the grease pits and gasoline tanks in the shop, there was no hope of saving the structure or anything in it. As the sun went down on this 28th day of July, flames still erupted with explosive force. It was scary, and yet, those of us who worked for Reemee could not leave. Suddenly, while watching, I felt a nudge at my elbow. Turning, I looked down into the pale, terror-filled face of Agnes . . . the tam pulled down over her ears.

"The wages of sin are death . . . and death is hell. I tell you, Hope, God has sent us hell in that fire. Look at the flames. Don't they tell you something? Don't they tell you that the world is coming to an end, and all those who don't obey Christ's wishes are doomed."

The whisper escalated until she was screaming her message. She seemed wild as she gesticulated, grimaced, held her arms above her head.

Quietly I slid away. She didn't notice. A small crowd was beginning to gather around her. I had a sinking feeling that the earth under her small, dainty feet was crumbling. That was the last time I saw her.

When we hadn't heard her admonishing voice for two or three days, we went into her room in the barrack. The bed was neatly made with Army sheets, pillows, blankets. Everything was in place. A Spartan brown rug was clean beside her bed. There was nothing in her clothes closet or dresser drawers. We heard she'd left her desk in the office the same way — empty and clean. Nobody saw her leave. Like a plunging star, she suddenly was just gone.

Chapter 18

The workshop fire tripled the workload in Blatchford's office. Lengthy lists of equipment and tools lost had to be assembled and typed. About thirty employees had lost valuable personal tools. Much Army equipment also had been reduced to scrap. Ottawa sent an officer — Capt. Ross Logan — to investigate the fire and replace all the losses. This meant that every man had to be interviewed so we could make a list of individual losses. Lists of Army equipment and tools (as listed in the shop at the time of the fire) had to be brought up to date, too. With the help of Logan we combined all lists, ordered everything from a supplier in Vancouver, and made arrangements for an early delivery by ship and rail.

Major Sarantos loaned us clerical help from the staff at headquarters so we could get the lists typed quickly.

The workshop was relocated to the refinery area. The big, cracking towers of the refinery had not been active since V-J Day. As I mentioned before, the U.S. government, fearing an attack by Japan, had built the refinery in 1943 and 1944. It had processed crude oil delivered 600 miles by the CANOL pipeline from Norman Wells, N.W.T. (CANOL is a coined word, an abbreviated linking of "Canada" and "oil.") The refinery had worked for nine months, but had been idle nearly two years when Reemee moved in. It had been listed for sale at $1 million with the U.S. War Surplus Property Agency.

The new workshop was three times bigger than the old one. While Mac and his men settled into their new surroundings, work went on in Blatchford's office. In six weeks tools were on their way, scheduled for delivery in Whitehorse on a Saturday. The shipment filled several railroad cars of the White Pass and Yukon Route. Ross Logan was pleased that the gigantic task of ordering these tools had been accomplished swiftly and without too much trouble. He was being optimistic too soon. The train went off the track thirty miles from Whitehorse, careened down the side of a mountain, and burst into flames. No one was hurt, but the tools

View from the Refinery Hill extends out over the area where Hope worked — in the first, closest long building. This picture was taken in 1948 or 1949, after the big towers and smoke stacks had been dismantled and trucked to Edmonton. Well outside the town of Whitehorse at that time, the refinery area was serviced by an Army bus.
Photo by James Quong.

were baked at such intense heat that all the temper in the steel was destroyed. Logan settled down to stay indefinitely in the north.

* * *

One day, shortly after the train wreck, Mac came into the office. It was just five o'clock, and everybody had left except me. He sat down heavily.

"I came to say 'goodbye'."

I wasn't surprised. I'd heard rumors he was leaving. Mac was an officer who had elected to switch over from the wartime Canadian Active Service Force to the Interim Force, a group that had been established to bridge the gap between the war years and the formation of a post-war Army. He seemed to me to be in that group of restless men who weren't sure if they wanted a full-time Army career or a kick at civvy street. Also, the Canadian Army was cutting its strength from half-a-million to 16,000 troops. Whether Mac had been caught in the "cut" along with scores of others was a matter for speculation.

He leaned back in his chair and nervously pulled at the corners of his moustache. "A new workshop officer is coming up. His name is Wally Ellis . . . and . . . oh, yes . . . Ted Gray from Headquarters will manage the radio station."

I felt sad. He'd been good to me when I had first arrived. "Where are you going?" I asked.

"Vancouver."

"Are you happy about leaving?"

He shrugged. "I don't know. Mixed feelings." He stood, reached out and shook my hand. "Good luck."

Somebody out on leave said he saw him in Vancouver the following year, driving a streetcar.

* * *

Rena and I had planned to go on vacation together in September, and one evening she said, "How would you like to help me document civilians in camps from Whitehorse to Dawson Creek?"

"I thought we'd planned to hitchhike?"

"I know, but this way we'll get a ride, in an Army car, expenses paid . . . to Dawson."

Vic, the Army private driver, drove the car. We were accompanied by Harry Gardiner, who was going out on posting, and Cpl. Al Hussey, pay clerk.

We stopped at every camp where civilians were working so that we could record names, correctly spelled, of employees, their unemployment insurance numbers, names of dependents and other data. The camps along the highway had posed a problem. Since pay cheques were issued in Whitehorse, it was difficult to keep an account of employees who were located hundreds of miles away in bush camps . . . employees who were often hired as seasonal labor. No authentic list of these workers had ever been made.

The weather was sunny and warm for my first trip south. Mountainsides and roadside ditches were covered with magenta purple fireweed, a wildflower that belongs to the evening primrose family

Marker for Mile Post 0, erected in 1946 on the main street of Dawson Creek, B.C., officially recognized the town as the starting point of the Alaska Highway. Whitehorse is located at Mile 917 — almost a thousand miles north of Dawson Creek.
Photo by James Quong.

and blooms in the late summer and autumn. In 1957 the fireweed was officially named floral emblem of the Yukon. We drove by an area that had been ravaged by forest fires the year before. The bleakness of the land was made even more grotesque by the odd charred skeleton of a branchless tree. And yet, a blanket of fireweed spread its color across the gutted area, hiding the worst of the devastation.

We stayed the first night in the officers' quarters (a mobile barrack unit) at Mile 670, where one steel bridge had been built and another was nearly finished. We had breakfast the following morning with Lieut. Bob Buckley and Sergeant-Major Keddell. Sgt. Dan Cameron was just leaving the mess hall as we walked in. I'd met him on my first skating venture in Whitehorse; he had taken me out for coffee that night and related a scary story of The Road. Cameron was in charge of heavy equipment at the bridge-building site. He talked for a few minutes, then went off to work.

By the time we arrived in Dawson Creek four days later, we were covered in dust from Army transports and equipment that stirred up the all-gravel road. The fine, powdery dust seeped through closed doors and windows; it made our dark brown hair look gray, our eyelashes look white.

Dawson Creek, where the Alaska Highway began, was called Mile 0. It was then a country town of about 3,000 people, the terminus for the Northern Alberta Railroad that ran through farmland, a distance of 525 miles, to the city of Edmonton. By the fall of 1948 the Hart Highway would link the town with Prince George, Prince Rupert and Vancouver via the Cariboo Road. The NWHS operated a freight warehouse and supply depot at Dawson Creek.

Just before we arrived at Mile 0 it began to rain. This cut down on the dust, but the churning mud in the farmers' fields and the grayness that suddenly settled in dampened our enthusiasm to hitchhike to Edmonton. Vic drove us back to Fort St. John, a distance of about 50 miles, where we phoned the airport to ask about a flight out. We were told an American transport plane was due in an hour, and, if we could be at the airport at that time, we'd get a lift to Edmonton.

Fort St. John was the home of Margaret "Ma" Murray, feisty editor of the weekly *Fort St. John Alaska Highway News.* Ma had become well-known through her hard-nosed, outspoken editorials and her personal items — brief reports of people who came and went, people who often did not want the world to know about their clandestine activities. Ma admitted that she was sometimes sued for libel, but this didn't prevent her from writing about life as it was. Ma's husband, George Murray, a veteran newspaperman, was elected to a seat in Parliament at Ottawa in 1949 as the member for the Cariboo district. Before that, he served at Victoria as a member of the Legislative Assembly for Lillooet, B.C. Ma's daughter Georgina, a journalist, had worked for the Canadian Broadcasting Corporation as a writer, and had done a stint in the Royal Canadian Navy during the war. Georgina Murray would come into my life at a later date, but on that rainy, muddy day when we waited for the transport plane to arrive, Rena and I thought only of getting out of that soggy, damp country.

* * *

I had not notified my dad that I was coming home. He was delighted to see me and we burned the candle at both ends talking about my experiences. He was shocked at the news of Tim's death. He'd enjoyed talking to Tim the few times he'd met him. War and politics had been the essence of their talks, giving Dad a re-run of his youthful experiences as an infantry officer in a Canadian regiment in another world war.

When I told Dad that I worked for Major Blatchford, he seemed especially interested. "Does Blatch hail from Edmonton?"

"Yes. Said he was born in Edmonton, educated here."

Dad considered this for a moment, then, very sadly said: "Edmonton had a mayor named Kenny Blatchford . . . back in the 1920s. He was one of the best mayors Edmonton ever had . . . promoted flying. As a matter of fact, the Edmonton airfield was named after him. 'Blatchford Field'."

Dad rose from his chair, went into the den and brought back a scrapbook he kept on historical events in Edmonton. He pointed to a clipping from the *Edmonton Bulletin*. "Ken Blatchford disappeared April 22, 1933, found in the river, dead of gunshot wounds — had been missing for months, believed suicide."

I was shocked. "Ken Blatchford must have been the major's father?"

Dad shrugged. "I don't know."

I couldn't help but think of this sad news at odd times while Rena and I hitchhiked across the northern states and crossed back into Canada at Windsor. I wondered if the two Blatchfords were related.

***

After visiting friends and relatives, and seeing the sights around Toronto and Montreal, we flew back to Whitehorse. Before I left the North, there were plans to move Blatchford's office into the refinery workshop. When I arrived back after my vacation, the office had been moved. My desk was near a large picture window that looked out across the flat plateau of the refinery grounds. I could see the mountains in the distance.

Helen Alexander had resigned and gone to live in Vancouver. A young soldier clerk named Eric Richard had arrived, and he was working with me. Two small offices joined the outer office where Eric and I worked. One of these rooms was Blatchford's office, and the other, we were told, would soon be occupied by Sgt.-Maj. Les Armstrong, who was being transferred from the Reemee workshop at Fort Nelson. A small hallway divided our offices from the two large workshop offices.

An eight-foot-high steel fence enclosed the 100 acres of refinery land. A custodian let us in at the gate.

102

***

The weather remained sunny in the daytime and cooler at night. At Forty-seven we had strung up a clothesline, running a rope from one poplar tree to another at the back of the barrack. One Sunday morning I went out to collect half-a-dozen pair of silk panties off the line and was stunned by what I saw. All the crotches of the pants had been ripped out. It looked as if a weird culprit had used a razor and had viciously mutilated each silk garment. Other women had washed the night before. (We had all chipped in on a small electric washing machine.) As I walked the length of the line I realized that all of the silk pants hung to dry the night before had been attacked with a sharp knife or razor. Betty had a dozen pair of panties made of real silk that she'd purchased on a trip to Paris, France. They, too, looked like jagged rags dancing in the breeze.

I'd been welcomed to Seventeen about a year before with a warning about peeping Toms. Now, again, a peeper was on the loose. Several of the women had seen the shadow of his face at a window, a shoulder slipping over the edge of a window frame, then hastily retreating. We called the RCMP (the Mounties) and reported the problem. Nobody was worried or afraid, but there was a strong, united determination to catch the culprit if the police did not catch him.

This steam engine pulled the train over the narrow-gauge railroad line from Whitehorse to Skagway, about ninety miles, in 1946. The White Pass and Yukon Railway later replaced this type of steam engine with diesel engines.
Photo by James Quong.

Chapter 19

Every time I heard a Norseman drone overhead I thought of Tim. Moments of nostalgia, grief. What would Tim think of my resolve to hike into The Valley on my own . . . a resolve that grew stronger, more exciting each day? I'd begun to read books on Yukon history in the hope of finding out more facts on Million Dollar Valley.

Whitehorse had a library housed in a small cabin behind the Whitehorse Inn. The library, a dark, rather dingy place, was operated by the IODE (Imperial Order Daughters of the Empire) on a volunteer basis, three days and three evenings a week. I soon learned that there was nothing on those dusty shelves about The Valley.

I searched through yellow, dog-eared back files of the *Whitehorse Star*, but again, I found nothing. The editor, Horace Moore, was a pipe-smoking, middle-aged man with Victorian morals whose journalistic style was confined largely to reporting on charity bazaars and tea parties. He had never heard of The Valley.

A friend introduced me to W.D. MacBride, district passenger representative for the White Pass and Yukon Route railroad. MacBride had a large, bright office that looked down on Main Street from the second floor of the train station. He was a thin, friendly man. He'd come to Whitehorse in 1914 and was close to retirement with the railroad when I met him.

He told me that The Valley of Lost Planes was tucked inside a remote, rugged section of the southeastern Yukon, but it really didn't interest him as much as Headless Valley in the Nahanni area of the Northwest Territories. Headless Valley had yielded headless corpses for half a century. Gold had lured men into this wild but beautiful land where hot springs bubbled from the earth and exotic waterfalls higher than Niagara fell from a plateau.

MacBride had written many stories about the North that had been published in national magazines. However, he had had nothing printed for about five years when I saw him.

W.D. MacBride, warmly clad in fur, stands in front of the Royal Mail Stage No. 9 in the MacBride Museum yard on First Avenue in Whitehorse. This photograph was taken in 1956.

Photo courtesy J. Hunston Collection/Yukon Archives.

"Editors aren't interested in the Yukon anymore. My stories come back, often not even read," he lamented.

MacBride's office walls were lined with bookcases that were full of rare books — some out of print. He loaned me *My Seventy Years* by Martha Louise Black, who had been elected to Parliament in Ottawa as the member for the Yukon in the 1930s. Mrs. Black lived in Whitehorse, just north of the railroad station. She was one of the few women who had hiked into the Klondike over the treacherous Chilkoot Pass in 1898. I read her book in one night. At a later date I would meet her in person.

Although I didn't find any books on The Valley in MacBride's office, I found something else . . . a gold mine of knowledge on the Yukon of another era. I began to get excited about the early history of the land when I read *Brother Here's a Man* by Kim Beattie — the story of Joe Boyle, who had made a million in the Klondike gold fields. In 1914 Boyle formed a Yukon regiment of sourdoughs whose buttons and insignia on their uniforms were made of Yukon gold. These hardy Northerners who were "dripping in gold" caused quite a sensation in London, England.

* * *

When I wasn't delving through MacBride's books, I was busy at Reemee. Blatchford's office had changed immensely since we'd moved to the refinery. Win Haines, a tall attractive Maritimer, and Sergeant-Major Armstrong had joined Eric Richard and me. The boxcars full of tools had arrived before Christmas and Reemee operations were back to normal, with Wally Ellis, a handsome, dark-haired man in his thirties, occupying MacKay's desk.

The Alaska Highway was opened to tourist travel in 1947. Previous to that there had been a ban on nonessential civilian vehicles, with the RCMP barring travellers at Mile 101. In the summer of '47 we began to see, moving along the road, trailers, buses converted into vacation units, and cars with supplies and camping gear heaped on top. Reemee was busy recovering tourist vehicles from ditches and gullies. One couple, going from Seattle to Alaska to settle, came down a steep hill too fast, turned car and trailer over and over until the trailer broke open, and spilled all their worldly wealth for a mile down the road.

"You gotta know how to drive this road," said Blatchford after seeing this wreck. "If a trailer catches up to you on one of these mountain hills, you better be prepared to do some fancy steering to avoid an accident."

Blatch was often absent from the office these days. We noticed he'd be on the job, bustling with energy and drive, for several months, then he'd be gone for a week and nobody could find him. After one such absence, he arrived at his desk looking tired and shaky. He was scheduled to go out to Edmonton in an Air Force plane due to leave in two hours. The RCAF had issued a memo weeks before, saying that passengers who arrived at the air terminal in a drunken state would not be permitted to board planes. The Air Force flew Army people, dependents, and civilians working for the Army back and forth to Edmonton and points in between. It was part of an agreement between the two services on takeover of the highway. We considered this transportation, which was free, a privilege, and none of us wanted to jeopardize it.

Blatchford called me into his office, told me he'd been "partying," and that he was worried he would not be accepted on the flight. I could smell booze. It was 9 a.m.

"You need a good strong cup of coffee," I suggested.

He shook his head. " I don't want a cup of coffee. Do you know what I want?"

I was young and naive, but I flung out a guess. "Scotch on the rocks?"

He sighed. His eyes were bloodshot, his whole being seemed to sag.

"Your wife and mother will be waiting in Edmonton. They can't come up without you," I reminded him. The Air Force had made a ruling that dependents must be accompanied on aircraft by a serviceman who was their next-of-kin.

He toyed with a paperweight on the desk for a few moments, then angrily he picked it up and dropped it with a thud. "People keep throwing up my dad to me."

I'd never mentioned his father to him, but he knew that I grew up in Edmonton and probably assumed I'd heard of the man.

"Your father . . . Ken Blatchford? Former mayor of Edmonton?"

He nodded.

"My dad told me he was one of the best mayors Edmonton ever had. I think you should be proud of him, tell any creeps who run your dad down to get lost."

He considered this a moment, then quietly said, "Thanks."

Somebody saw him having breakfast later in the Klondyke Cafe, just before he boarded the plane.

* * *

The Army operated a diesel bus every thirty minutes, and no fares were required. The bus made a tour of the town of Whitehorse, went up the refinery hill, toured the Army married quarters, the air base, the Air Force married quarters, and came back down to lower Whitehorse. Twice a day, at 7:30 a.m. and 5 p.m., the bus took Reemee employees to and from work in the refinery area.

In the autumn of 1947, the Army decided to withdraw the bus from the refinery. Top brass felt it was the responsibility of the workers to arrange their own transportation.

Ninety-nine percent of the Reemee employees had no mode of transportation other than the bus and taxis. One lad drove a motorcycle and another had a beat-up surplus jeep he had purchased in Edmonton. There weren't any car salesmen in Whitehorse. The only place we could purchase cars was at War Assets, a government concern that sold war surplus material. Used army cars, jeeps and pickups were priced so high at War

Assets that few individuals made purchases.

The withdrawal of bus service caused discontent among the workers. They did not like to hitchhike to work, and taxis were too expensive. One day the civilians decided that they were not going to work until the bus was reinstated. They sat on the steps and sidewalk outside the mess hall one morning at eight o'clock. By ten o'clock word of the "strike" had filtered into the brigadier's office. He sent one of his administrative officers out to talk to the men. By 10:30 a.m., a half-hour later, bus service to the refinery was reinstated.

This was the only sit-down strike encountered by the Northwest Highway System. The Army was suddenly confronted by a mixed establishment . . . military personnel who had to take orders from senior officers and civilians who did not have to take orders from anybody.

* * *

In January, 1948, Brigadier Walsh left on posting to Germany and Brig. A.B. Connelly arrived to become the second commander of the NWHS. Connelly, at forty, was a thin man of medium height who kept a low profile, and yet, like Walsh, he had had a distinguished career. He had been educated at the Royal Military College of Canada, commissioned as a lieutenant, Royal Canadian Engineers, on May 18, 1931. He was general staff officer 2, 1st Canadian Corps in 1941, and was promoted to lieutenant colonel that year; served as chief, Royal Canadian Engineers, 4th Canadian Armoured Division in 1942 and 1943; and was promoted to acting brigadier on June 23, 1943. He was chief engineer, 1st Canadian Corps, June 23, 1943, to July 26, 1944; took command of Headquarters, "B" Group, Canadian Reinforcement Unit on September 8, 1944; was commander, Canadian troops, Northwest Europe, in July, 1946; was deputy chief of general staff and deputy adjutant-general, Canadian Military Headquarters, London, England, 1946.

Shortly after Connelly's arrival in Whitehorse, he dressed in civilian clothes and visited the sergeants' mess. In a back room, a game of pool was in progress. Connelly stepped in to watch the game. One of the players turned abruptly, raised his cue over the newcomer's head and brought it down hard. The quick action of an onlooker who caught the stick in midair saved the brigadier's head.

The incident was the talk of the camp, but, after an inquiry, nothing seemed to happen. A young woman who took shorthand notes at the hearing said that witnesses saw nothing and the cue swinger remembered nothing.

* * *

The winter of 1947 to 1948 was not as cold as the previous winter. Although snow piled up around the Army barracks and the wind often howled a dirge, we skied every weekend — crossing the river on the ice, climbing up and slaloming down the slopes.

In January the bridge-building crews from No. 1 Road hit town. There had been much talk for a month about a birthday party for John Osterdahl, a sergeant. When the evening of the party finally arrived, only Tudy and I, of the fourteen women in the barrack, had not been invited.

Osterdahl, in his forties, had been a sailor during the war. A tall, craggy Swede, his most famous saying was: "It took me ten years to learn to say 'jug' instead of 'yug', and then they changed it to 'crock'."

About ten o'clock, when I'd just had a shower and washed my hair, Bob Buckley and Rena came over to ask me to come to the party. "There's somebody wants to see you," they said.

I told them that the "somebody" could come over to see me, but they wouldn't listen. "It's a good party. Come on," they urged.

Finally, in gabardine slacks and sweater, with wet hair, and muffled up in a parka, I joined them. We walked the two blocks to the sergeants' lounge. The place was full, with people dancing to a Wurlitzer, and Osterdahl, surrounded by a group, telling stories of his sailor days. Buckley said that one person was missing — Jim Keddell, a six-footer who was big enough to wrestle a bull moose to the ground. Keddell had been married the day before, in Fort St. John. Ma Murray's daughter, Georgina, had become Mrs. Keddell, and, in the early spring, the newlyweds would come to Whitehorse to live.

Al LeClair, the self-appointed "Frog" I'd met on my first day, was slinging out drinks at the bar, where a group of male barflies always seemed to hang out. One of them broke away and joined us.

"Remember me?" he said.

"Sure. Dan Cameron."

"You've got a good memory. It's great to see you again," he told me.

He bought me a drink. We danced, sang, had birthday cake, tossed balloons in the air. A fight broke out, but the delinquents were ushered outside by two self-appointed bouncers and were taken home. In a strange, bizarre way, the fight added an exciting finale to an exciting birthday party, and at four o'clock in the morning a dozen of us went to the Whitehorse Inn to talk and sober up on coffee.

"Can I see you tomorrow night?" asked Dan.

"I thought you said you had to go to Six-seventy? You're closing the camp, moving stuff to Whitehorse?"

"Sure, but I'll be back. Eight o'clock?"

"Awright."

"And what about the night after that and the night after that?"

He was a charmer, often presenting a sort of swashbuckling image. And yet, he was a loner, too, and an adventurer, this Dan Cameron who hailed from Glengarry County in Ontario. He'd been twice mentioned in dispatches during the war, for special services beyond the call of duty. He had enlisted with the Stormont, Dundas and Glengarry Highland Regiment, Canadian Army, as a teen-ager in 1939.

"I was one of half-a-dozen soldiers who guarded Lock 22 near Dickinson's Landing, fifteen miles west of Cornwall, Ontario. I'm talking about the Canadian side of the St. Lawrence River now . . . that was the winter of 1939 to 1940. We wore kilts with long underwear. Some sight. It seems the government had the crazy idea the Germans might come down the river and blow up the locks. One look at us in kilts, with underwear showing down to our ankles, would have been enough to send them back to Germany by the quickest route."

I loved to listen to him talk. He had a knack of punctuating every story with the right touch of humor and pathos.

He had four brothers and four sisters. "I'm wedged right in the middle," he often said, "four older, four younger."

Four of the Cameron boys were overseas at the same time in the thick of fighting in Italy, Holland, France and Germany, And . . . all four came back to Canada without a scratch, "older, wiser, hating war."

Chapter 20

My second Christmas in the Yukon was quieter than the first one. I lounged away four days, including Christmas Day, in the hospital where I was isolated with a strep throat. Carollers came and went outside my door, and a nurse dropped in occasionally to give me a shot of penicillin.

Although I didn't relish this kind of Christmas vacation, I *was* able to see the military hospital from the inside looking out, instead of the outside looking in. We civilians were given free medical and dental care by the Army, which was a tremendous boost to our morale. There was a small, frame, frontier-type hospital in downtown Whitehorse, but we had often heard that costs for accommodation and care were astronomical, and none of us had any medical insurance coverage.

By the time Christmas day dawned, I was feeling better and was able to eat a turkey dinner supplied by the cooking staff in the nearby mess hall. A tall, angular nursing sister, wearing the trim veil of a military nurse and lieutenant's pips on the shoulders of her hospital uniform, was on duty that day.

"You couldn't swing a gopher in one of these rooms," she said, stepping in and popping a thermometer into my mouth.

I nodded in agreement, studying the hospital bed, wedged in between two walls with a white metal bedside table and single chair. The walls were unpainted and splintery. The single window, which could be opened by shoving the bottom up, was stuck shut with ice and snow. Jack Frost had painted an abstract picture across the glass. It reminded me of a burst of fireworks.

Outside my door was a maze of corridors where jutting signs told the location of bathrooms, offices, operating theatre, X-ray unit, pediatric and physiotherapy departments, dental area, maternity.

The nursing sister came back later that night and sat at the foot of my bed.

"You'll be able to go tomorrow, you lucky skunk," she said. "The joint's full. You wouldn't believe . . . we've got kids with measles, alcoholics drying out, and babies — five this month. The full moon brings out the pregnant women."

"How many people can you pack in here?" I asked.

"It's a fifty-bed hospital, but we can accommodate sixty people quite easily." She sighed and studied the bare walls and the bare wooden floor. "Every winter we have problems. Water pipes and rads burst at the rate of one every three days. Floors heave, and if windows are opened, the steam pipes freeze. If windows are kept shut, the building gets so hot and dry we can hardly breathe."

"The hospital was built by the American army?"

"Yeah. In forty-two, as a temporary measure only. So . . . it's six years old now."

"What about fires?" I asked, since fire was always a threat in the camp.

"Last month we had a fire in the hospital power plant. We thought we'd have to evacuate patients, but it wasn't necessary because the fire department was right on the job and the boilers didn't have a chance to cool off enough to put us in danger. But . . . we found out an interesting thing."

She paused to light a cigarette, and I jumped in with a question. "That, with a bad fire, the power supply to the hospital might be cut off?"

"Exactly. We have an auxiliary generating plant for the operating room, but it's located in the boiler house. There's just no other suitable place for it."

"Wow. So you could find yourself in the dark in the middle of an operation if there were a power failure?"

"Something like that. But, get this."

"What?"

"We've indented for a number of mantle lamps for emergency lighting in the operating room."

"You mean coal oil lamps?"

"Coal oil or gasoline. That puts us into the pioneer category, doesn't it?"

We laughed, picturing the old-fashioned lamps swinging above a modern operating table with masked doctors and nurses struggling to see if they were in the general area of an appendix. She was in a talkative mood, and before she left I asked her what the hospital did to help alcoholics. The night before, an alcoholic had kept those of us in that particular wing awake half the night. He'd screamed in a pathetic, weird pleading wail for a drink. "Just one, dammit . . . just one."

"We don't like treating alcoholics. We're really not geared to that kind of thing. Drying out is painful."

113

On that note, she left to work on charts.

I got out of the hospital in time to celebrate Boxing Day, December 26, with a quiet party at Forty-seven. On New Year's Eve, Dan and I rang in 1948 at a formal dance at the sergeants' mess. About a hundred of us clinked our glasses and sang out lustily to the beat of a tinny piano, "And here's a hand my trusty frien', and gie's a hand o' thine . . . we'll tak' a cup o' kindness yet . . . for auld lang syne."

A straggly line of Canadian soldiers marches to a church parade on Christmas Day in 1947.

Chapter 21

An avalanche of foot soldiers arrived in January for winter training. The PPCLI (Princess Patricia's Canadian Light Infantry, often called "Princess Pats") marched into our midst with pressed uniforms, polished boots, smart salutes, taps and reveille.

The Alaska Highway soldier, operating cranes and slide rules, fighting mud, swamps, mosquitoes, frostbite, and swollen rivers, and up to his armpits in grease to keep decrepit machinery working — this soldier had little time or need for boot polish and salutes.

The Princess Pats were billeted in old, unused American Army barracks. When I walked to work, I often saw these soldiers lining up in a parade square near the barracks area — packs on their backs, ready to hit the trail for the day. When they were in camp they ate in our mess hall, and we were fascinated with the precise way they marched in for meals, a corporal out front calling out commands. The local soldiers straggled in at odd hours, slunk into the nearest chairs at the nearest tables, ate and were gone. Although these NWHS soldiers seemed unhappy with the invasion of the infantry, we women enjoyed the diversion. Four sergeants who were members of the advance party for the PPCLI adopted Forty-seven as a second home. They came over in the evenings to play cards, talk, enjoy an odd joke. Often they brought coffee, bread and cold meat from their rations so we could have a late-night snack.

Three handsome PPCLI officers dated Betty, Rena and me. We often went over to the officers' mess, a square, rather pretentious building next-door to Forty-seven. The dance floor of maple was highly polished; soft lights, coffee tables, scatter rugs, and books gave a homey atmosphere; a pool room offered challenges; a mahogany bar with indirect lighting added style. For formal parties a band played dance music, but on ordinary evenings Dal Hull, who had replaced Gardiner as paymaster, could often be found at the piano where he entertained us by imitating Fats

Waller. Hull was popular with everybody, and especially liked by the half-dozen pay clerks on staff in the pay office. Shortly after he'd arrived, he'd put through long overdue raises in salaries for most of them. I found that he had a certain charisma which attracted people to him and made them feel at ease.

"He sure is a great guy, wonderful to work with," said Rena.

At the piano, Hull — a rotund little man in his late thirties — imitated to perfection the nasal baritone and jive patter of Waller. We were thrilled as we listened to "Ain't Misbehavin'," "Honeysuckle Rose," "I've Got a Feelin' I'm Fallin'." They were halcyon days. We didn't know then that tragedy lay ahead for Hull, that in a year he would be transferred to Chilliwack, B.C., and rumors would spread that he was suspected of dipping his fingers into the till of the Army pay office. It wouldn't be until two years later that we would learn the truth in a supplement to Canadian Army Orders, dated April 10, 1950, at Ottawa:

> ZP2658 Captain Arthur Edward Dallas Hull, Royal Canadian Army Pay Corps, Western Command Pay Office, an officer of the Canadian Army Active Force, attached for all purposes to the Royal Canadian School of Military Engineering, Chilliwack, British Columbia, was tried by General Court Martial at Chilliwack, B.C. on 18 January 1950 on three charges under Section 17 of the Army Act relating to misapplication of public property.
>
> Captain A.E.D. Hull pleaded guilty to all three charges, was found guilty on all three charges and was sentenced to be cashiered (out of the Army) and to be imprisoned with hard labor for one year.
>
> The finding and sentence having been duly confirmed by the Governor General in Council, the charges, finding and sentence were duly promulgated on the 6th day of March 1950.

In January and February 1948, however, we and our PPCLI escorts, unaware of the impending tragedy, laughed, sang and made merry as Hull performed in traditional Fats Waller style at the piano in the officers' mess.

* * *

When carnival time drew near once again, the men in the Reemee shop asked if they could nominate me as a candidate for carnival queen. I was delighted they had thought of me, but I suggested they nominate Rena, who, as personnel director, knew more people than I. Rena was also more of an extrovert than I. She was an excellent sportswoman who had played professional basketball in Edmonton, and who could bat a ball into the backfield at a softball game. She could play the bagpipes, too, although we didn't encourage that kind of "noise" in Forty-seven. She and I often kidded one another about the Irish and the Scots. Since my mother had been born and reared in Cork City, Eire, I felt a certain loyalty to the Irish. Rena's parents had emigrated to Canada from Scotland. Our Whitehorse basketball team was called "The Shamrocks." We were given big green shamrocks to sew on our white sweatshirts.

"I'll sew a shamrock on the seat of my shorts where it belongs," Rena said one night with a mischievous twinkle in her eye.

"And sure, 'twould be easier to sit on than the thistle," I replied.

We played basketball twice a week in one of the Air Force hangars — a cavernous deep freeze. Rena could shoot a ball from centre floor and hit the basket with a ringer. We played a rough, tough game because we were challenged by a town team that played rough and tough and played to win.

Our new PPCLI friends threw their weight behind Rena for carnival queen. They had brought two Army tanks to Whitehorse, a part of their training gear, and they decorated one tank with a slightly misspelled message in huge red letters — QUEEN RENE!

The following week, engineers from 17 Works Company, RCE, nominated one of their stenographers for carnival queen, thus splitting the Army vote. Although the RCAF stood behind their nominee — an attractive switchboard operator — they didn't have the numbers needed for a win. A tall, brunette woman sponsored by the merchants in Whitehorse reigned that year. The town had backed her solidly. I couldn't help but feel a pang of jealousy when I saw her, standing on a podium at the carnival, all wrapped up in one of the prizes — a mink coat.

Again, there were the kangaroo courts, dog races on the river, dance-hall girls, laughter and song. I remembered, with a stab of loneliness, how Tim had stepped into my life on the last high note of the carnival the year before, and how a few months later he had taken wing with "the other woman" and had never come back. My heart shrivelled up a little until I remembered that I had a mission — to see The Valley that had once captured his imagination — The Valley that lay somewhere in the far reaches of the land.

***

The week after the carnival, an angry confrontation between a sergeant with No. 1 Road and a PPCLI officer sent rumors buzzing from Mile 0 to the Alaska border. Major Blatchford broke the news in our office. He studied me, his astute look rather piercing under shaggy, knit brows.

"Cameron's in trouble. Refused to salute a Pat."

Win Haines and I stared at him.

"What kind of trouble?" I finally blurted out.

"There's rumor the officer's going to lay a charge."

"For not saluting?" I asked, incredulous.

Blatch grew red in the face. "I don't know why they don't billet those little tin soldiers ten miles away, instead of right under our noses."

Blatch liked Dan. After he heard that I'd been seen with him several times at the centre, the sergeants' mess, and the ski hills, he paused while dictating letters to me one afternoon. "He's a good lad, that Cameron. Knows machinery . . . diesel, gas engines, you name it. And . . . he's a worker, too."

"Also, in spite of being a fourth-generation Scot, he's stubborn as a mule," I added.

I thought of the stubborn streak when I heard about the salute problem.

The engineers from No. 1 Road had been attending a school on Caterpillar tractors which had been held one week in February at the Army theatre. The "trouble" had erupted in the middle of that school week.

Rumor had it Dan was in jail. The Army used the RCMP jail, located a little south of the headquarters building and behind the Army PX. In the summer, when we walked past the open, barred windows, the prisoners (who could be incarcerated for a maximum of only two years less a day) would wave and call to us. In most instances we knew them — civilians or soldiers who had gotten into brawls, or had been picked up as being drunk and disorderly. One Reemee civilian spent six months in the jail. His greatest problem was gambling at the Ace-Away games, and suddenly he found himself in debt to the tune of $10,000.

One day Dan walked into Forty-seven. Tudy, Rena and I were talking and listening to the radio in the reception room. We greeted him like a hero.

"Thought you were in jail?"

"Not yet," he murmured.

"Sit down. What happened? For Gawd's sake . . . rumors have been flying."

Somebody rushed to get him a coffee.

"Well, it shouldn't have happened, really. I guess, between the officer and me, temper got in the way." he began; then he told us how he was the last of about fifty engineers hurrying over to the Army theatre for the Cat school at eight o'clock that particular morning. Although the thermometer registered 5 below zero and snow lay everywhere, Dan was dressed in Army fatigues and brogues — no parka, no snow boots.

"I saw this group of Pats on skis, assembling outside one of the huts. I didn't pay too much attention to them until I heard a gruff voice calling, 'Sergeant . . . sergeant . . . come here'. I walked over to this tall Pat who was all bundled up in a ski suit. He told me that all morning he'd seen soldiers crossing his parade square and not one of them had saluted him. 'Don't you salute your officers here in the Yukon?' he asked. I studied the ski attire the man was wearing, and said, yes . . . we salute an officer when we recognize one."

Rena and I laughed. "They all look alike — like Eskimos — in those ski outfits," she said.

"Well . . . the Pat turned," continued Dan. "On the back of his parka a captain's insignia was plainly visible. He faced me again. 'You don't deserve to wear those ribbons on your tunic.' "

Dan paused, lit a cigarette. "I'm damn proud of those ribbons," he said finally, pointing to the array of six ribbons and one oak leaf on his tunic. This young punk showed me two ribbons that he'd earned — somewhere. I'd been all primed to give him a damn salute until he mentioned my medals. I turned and walked away, but a PPCLI sergeant caught up with me to get my name and regimental number."

Fifteen minutes later a messenger tapped Dan on the shoulder while he listened to the lecturer at the school.

"The major wants to see you immediately. What the hell have you done? The Old Man's wild."

Major Lovatt Fraser asked for an explanation of the morning's incident, and when Dan told him that he was all primed to give the Pat a salute until he heard the words, "You don't deserve to wear those ribbons on your tunic," Lovatt-Fraser shouted, "He said *that?*"

There was a pause while the major walked over to the window and looked out at the snow and the distant mountain peaks. Then he came back to his desk with an angry stride. "These Pats can go home anytime as far as I'm concerned," he growled, then left to talk to the senior highway engineer — Lieutenant-Colonel Jones.

The following day Lovatt-Fraser called Dan into his office and told him the Pat officer had decided it was best to drop the charge of insubordination.

Life settled back to normal. February bowed out like a lamb — the mercury climbing overnight from 10 below to 30 above. In my new quarters in Forty-seven, the oil furnaces had hummed through January, February, March, April. Tap water had run. Yet, in this comfort, I could not forget the previous winter that had forged me into a tough pioneer.

The Donjek River bridge with its eight 200-foot steel spans was built between 1949 and 1952. This bridge was one of the biggest projects of its type undertaken by Canadian Army Engineers on the Alaska Highway.
Photo by James Quong.

Chapter 22

Early that spring No. 1 Road relocated at Mile 1130, where the Army was getting ready to place eight 200-foot steel bridge spans over the Donjek River. Dan Cameron and Jim Keddell were in the advance party setting up camp at this location 210 miles northwest of Whitehorse.

In March, Georgina Murray Keddell arrived from Fort St. John. She and Jim moved all their worldly wealth into Army Cemesto No. 13 — a small, prefab bungalow set in a row of identical bungalows in the married quarters in upper Whitehorse.

Dan and Jim tried to get into town on an odd weekend. One Friday night, as we walked to Forty-seven following a dance at the sergeants' mess, Dan told me we were invited to visit the Keddells in Cemesto 13 the following evening. Although I didn't know Georgina, I knew of her mother, Ma Murray, the outspoken editor of the *Alaska Highway News* in Fort St. John.

I had not met Ma, but she and I had mutual friends. One young reporter who helped her get her paper together once a week told me that two of her many pet sayings were, "Rare as tits on a bull," and, "That's for damshur."

When Fort St. John was bursting with U.S. soldiers and civilians building the highway, Ma launched her weekly paper with a special "personal" column that listed people who were registered at the local hotels. It was rumored that this column touched off seven divorces in a year.

Prior to moving to Fort St. John in 1942, Ma had been editor and publisher of the *Bridge River Lillooet News* in Lillooet, B.C. On the upper left-hand corner of the editorial page she published the following message, with the circulation figures changing from one week to the next: "Bridge River Lillooet News. Printed in the Sagebrush Country of the Lillooet every Thursday, God willing. Guarantees a chuckle every week and a belly laugh once a month or your money back. Subscriptions $5.00 in Canada. Furriners $6.00. This week's circulation 1,769 and every bloody one of them paid for."

George Murray, Georgina's father, was the managing editor of the *Vancouver Sun* in the late 1920s and early '30s, and in 1933 was elected a Liberal member of the legislature for Lillooet.

* * *

I'd heard Jim was a big man, but when we arrived at Cemesto 13 and he opened the door to our knock, I was surprised at the moustached six-footer who weighed all of 300 pounds. Georgina, about five-foot six, was also big in a buxom way.

"We two present a bold front," she said, laughing, as they led us into their comfortably furnished living room.

She had bright brown eyes and a friendly smile. She had worked as a scriptwriter for the Canadian Broadcasting Corporation, and had done public relations work when she was in the Navy during the Second World War. I was quite impressed with her background in writing and we warmed up to one another immediately. Within weeks, she had a job as a reporter on the weekly *Whitehorse Star.*

Dan and Jim had crossed paths in England during the war. That night, with tongue in cheek, they told us how Dan had dated Ann, a young Englishwoman whose mother owned a couple of thoroughbred horses.

"Ann and I used to take the horses out for exercise, around the English countryside," said Dan.

Jim dated Ann's mother, and, although he and Dan were aware of one another in England, they had never met, face to face, until they joined No. 1 Road in the Yukon, where they began to compare notes.

That spring, Dan and I often met the Keddells for a movie or a drink at the sergeants' mess. When the men were at the Donjek, Georgina and I had evening dinner at the Whitehorse Inn now and then. On one such occasion she came to the inn with a copy of the *Star* tucked under her arm. While we waited for our dinner she unfolded the paper and showed me an article written by a man who had applied for a job as a sanitary inspector for Whitehorse. The Territorial Government had chosen one person for the job from several applications. This man had been one of the rejects. He had been bitter about the turn of events, and the article he wrote outlined what he thought of Whitehorse.

"Hot off the press, and unabridged," said Georgina as she handed me the paper.

The man said that a person could walk down the streets of Whitehorse any time of the day or night, and expect to dodge slops as people leaned out from their doors and heaved. There were no garbage laws, no sewage systems. He compared the town to Paris in the 1500s.

* * *

In the winter and spring of 1948, work went on as usual at Reemee. In a month-end report for April, 1948, Blatchford said the following: "Special-manufacture jobs during the month consisted of the making of 65 pile points for road maintenance, manufacture of special pullers for Hercules Diesel Motors, and the loan of a body-repair man to the RCAF for six days to do repair work on the landing-gear doors of a Beechcraft airplane. A normal number of recovery jobs were completed during the month, one an emergency when two fighter aircraft — Mustangs — crashed on landing."

In another report, it was noted that Reemee spent four hours sharpening surgical instruments for the military hospital operating room.

In January, 1948, 100 men from the W.M. Barnes Co. of Los Angeles, engineers and contractors, arrived in Whitehorse. Imperial Oil Ltd. had purchased the refinery and signed a contract with Barnes to dismantle the smoke stacks, towers, and ninety-foot-high power plant, and take the whole assembly, piece by piece, to Edmonton, 1,350 miles away.

When Imperial launched the Discovery Well at Leduc on February 13, 1947, the oil age in Alberta was ushered in with a roar. Subsequent wells pointed up the need for a refinery to process crude oil. There was a general shortage of building materials after the war, and Imperial decided to dismantle the Whitehorse refinery and set it up again at a site east of Edmonton.

The plan called for ten of the largest diesel tractors in the world to move night and day between Whitehorse and Dawson Creek, a distance of 917 miles. At Dawson Creek, the giant loads would be shifted to railroad cars to continue their journey to Edmonton.

Each massive vehicle weighed nearly twenty tons when empty, and the largest had twenty-one forward speeds. As they wended their way south over mountain summits, hair-pin turns and fragile wooden bridges, each carried 60- to 100-ton loads.

At Teslin Lake a 2,326-foot wooden bridge was condemned by Barnes's engineers, who found it was not sturdy enough to carry these enormous loads. An ice-bridge was built — no easy feat. Snow was cleared in a wide path from shore to shore on that particular arm of the lake; holes were dug in the nearby ice; and pumps poured water from the lake into the snowbanked trench. This operation took a week, while engineers built the ice up, inch by inch, until it was thick enough to bear the heaviest loads.

When the sun sank behind the winter horizon, I could look out the Reemee office window and see sparks moving back and forth, up and down and crosswise, against the black velvet backdrop of sky. Oxyacetylene torches were busy night and day cutting down towers as high as 146 feet. This was a spectacular sight after dark (close to five o'clock on a winter's afternoon) . . . like tiny, gold tracer bullets moving around in outer space. A medley of stars.

We, in Reemee, were in the heart of the activity as the roar of tractors and cranes, the shouts of crew foremen, the sizzle of welders' cutting tools and the hiss of oxyacetylene torches echoed and blended across the refinery area.

Supervisors and foremen from Barnes's operation often came into our office to confer with Blatchford in the hope of solving road problems, which were enormous. Each big diesel unit was equipped with twenty massive tires, the eight driving tires needing chains for traction on ice and snow. Tire punctures occurred frequently in that wilderness, where the nearest garage was 400 miles away. Also, the whole transfer operation had to be delayed until the gravel roadbed of the highway was frozen enough to withstand the loads.

American drivers, hired to bring the units from California, went back to the States after one or two trips on the highway. Many of them, we judged from their remarks, were sure the Alaska Military Road led straight to hell. Canadian drivers were hired to replace them.

One of the biggest problems encountered was at the refinery gate when units tried to manipulate the narrow turn to go up the refinery hill. As a driver drove up to the gate to leave with his load, he faced a solid hill that met the narrow gravel road on the far side at a ninety-degree angle. Most outfits jacknifed on this turn. It took a lot of horsepower and know-how to get them straightened out and on their way.

One afternoon, after meeting with Einar, a Barnes supervisor, Blatchford stopped by my desk. He told me Einar had asked him to recommend a Canadian who could supervise the big units along the road — a top man who knew big diesels and the road like a Methodist preacher knew his Bible.

"I told him there's only one man with all that know-how, and that man is Dan Cameron," Blatch said.

*Ice created dangerous conditions on the treacherous hill
that goes up and over Steamboat Mountain. An Army road
grader is shown breaking up the ice caused by run-off
overflowing the ditch. The W.M. Barnes Co. of Los Angeles,
hired to dismantle the Whitehorse refinery and transport
tons of refinery equipment to Edmonton, encountered
numerous problems on these icy hills.*
Photo by James Quong.

A few days later Dan called me from the Donjek. Barnes had
contacted him. They offered him $1,000 a month and a
brand-new pickup truck of his own if he took the job to supervise the moving of this gigantic machinery from Whitehorse to
Dawson Creek. They also told him they were negotiating with the
Army to arrange for his "loan" for about a three-month period
— February to April.

"You don't sound excited about the offer," I told him on the
phone.

"Well . . . I'm flattered that they think I'm the best man for the
job. It's a boost to my ego, but . . . I don't like decisions. You
see . . . I'm due for a six weeks' leave any day now."

The engineers took vacations in the wintertime so they could
be on the job in spring, summer and autumn when the weather

125

*At Nisutlin Bay (an arm of Teslin Lake), a transport tractor
fell through the deck of the original wooden bridge, built by
the U.S. Army in 1942. This bridge was the longest (2,326
feet) timber trestle bridge on the entire highway. U.S. Army
Engineers repaired the bridge by driving piles through the
tractor resting on the bottom of the bay. In the meantime,
an improvised raft took traffic across the bay, as shown in
this photo. In the 1970s, after a new steel bridge had been
built, an enterprising Canadian retrieved the transport
tractor from the bottom of the bay, made it run, and
operated it in the vicinity for several years.*
Photo by James Quong.

was right for road projects and bridge building.

The following weekend, after the telephone conversation, Dan
came to town. We went skiing, trying for the first time a ski run
the Air Force had bulldozed down the side of a mountain a mile
north of the airport and west of the highway. The run was rough,
but it was a challenge for amateur skiers like us. While having
a sandwich later at the Klondyke, Dan told me he had turned
down the Barnes offer, that he felt he owed himself a vacation
and that he would be flying out the following day to go home to
Cornwall, Ontario, where he would see his mother, father, sisters
and brothers.

Einar, a quiet man with a slight Norwegian accent, told me later that Barnes was disappointed Dan hadn't taken the job. A civilian working for the Army, who did not have the same high recommendations, took on the arduous task of making sure the big units reached their destinations. These units had rolled up half a million miles when the last length of pipe and the last big stack were delivered at Dawson Creek. A total of 7,000 tons of equipment had been moved, at a cost well over $7 million.

Chapter 23

Einar fascinated me. He was a soft-spoken man in his early forties — a man of medium height, powerfully built with broad shoulders. When wearing a fur-trimmed parka and fur cap, he often looked Slavic — his face leathery from so much time spent out-of-doors, laughter lines etched into the skin at the corners of the blue eyes.

On winter afternoons I saw Einar skiing during his lunch break, across the flat plateau of refinery grounds. He skied with easy grace, like a professional.

John Oliver, city editor at the *Edmonton Bulletin* in the 1940s, once told me I had an excellent "nose" for news. John had also told me he'd buy any feature articles I wanted to send his way from the North — at the going rate. I sensed there was a story in Einar, yet when I tried to talk to him about his life he quietly, courteously, changed the subject. Then Blatch told me Einar had won the American cross-country ski competition the year before, and had won firsts at competitions in Europe, including the Olympics.

I belonged to the Whitehorse ski club, and we were trying to find someone who was proficient enough in the slalom to teach us for a couple of hours on Sunday afternoons. One day I grew bold and asked Einar if he would give us instructions the following Sunday. I was surprised and elated when he said he would. I imagined how impressed my friends at the ski hill would be when I turned up with this Olympic champ, and also . . . I would learn more about him, would do a story on the dismantling of the refinery and work into it a story on Einar the man.

The following Sunday he picked me up, skis and all, in a Barnes truck. We left the vehicle parked by the highway and skied the two miles in to the run. At the hill, my friends *were* impressed as he demonstrated, like a champ, how best to do difficult turns on the run, and how best to handle skis while doing the slalom. When somebody asked how long he had been skiing, he replied modestly, "I skied before I walked."

Once, he pointed to distant sun-washed mountain peaks outlined against the sky. "That's where I want to be," he said. "In the high places."

When I tried to talk to him about his life during the war, he carefully led me back to the current topic — skiing. I felt exasperated, and one day I said to Blatch, "Einar interests me. Do you know anything about his life?"

Blatch, a little stunned, looked at me. "You haven't heard Einar's story?"

"How could I have heard when he never talks about himself . . . never even reveals his last name?"

"He was written up in *The Reader's Digest* a few years ago. I have a copy. I'll bring it to the office tomorrow."

The following day I found the November, 1946, issue of *The Reader's Digest* on my desk, with a note clipped to the cover: "Hope . . . read page 25 . . . 'Eleven Against the Nazi A-Bomb'."

That evening, curled up on my bunk, I excitedly read the story of Einar. It began thus:

One morning in February, 1944, the heavily laden railroad ferry *Hydro* was plunging through the choppy waves of Norway's Lake Tinnsjo. Suddenly — the dull boom of an explosion below decks. The ship lurched, shuddered to a stop. Five minutes later the *Hydro* had sunk, and with it Hitler's dream of possessing the first atom bomb. Behind that explosion lies the story of one of the war's most fantastic undercover operations.[1]

The article, written by Frederic Sondern, Jr., and condensed from *The Minneapolis Tribune*, told how the Germans had ordered the Norwegian electrochemical plant Norsk Hydro, near the village of Vermork, to increase its production of deuterium oxide (heavy water) — a chemical essential in the making of the atom bomb. The British War Cabinet gave top priority to a plan to destroy the heavy water at the Norsk plant.

Because of the high, treacherous mountains in the area, the cabinet said it would not be practical to launch a bombing attack by the Royal Air Force. They were looking at a commando job.

[Early in the war] . . . a group of Norwegian resistance men had seized coastal steamer *Galtesund* and sailed her through the mine and submarine perils of the North Sea into Aberdeen. One of these men was a hydro-electrical specialist who had already organized a highly effective section of the

129

Norwegian underground. Einar (he and his colleagues prefer not to have their last names revealed) was immediately summoned to Special Forces headquarters in London.[2]

The Norsk Hydro plant was a seven-story steel and concrete building perched on the top of a 1,000-foot cliff. All approaches were heavily guarded by Gestapo soldiers. In spite of this, operations "Swallow" and "Gunnerside" were born in England. Einar — a one-man advance party — was dropped from an RAF bomber on a moonlit night, into the mountains thirty miles from Norsk and Vermork where he was born and grew up, and where his brothers, sisters and parents still lived. With the help of a brother, he obtained a job at the plant. Within weeks he reported to British Intelligence that the Germans had speeded up the production of deuterium oxide. The war cabinet ordered a commando assault at once.

Four carefully chosen Norwegians called "Swallows," all expert skiers, were dropped in October, 1942, into the mountains to reinforce Einar. Treacherous air currents carried the men 100 miles off-target.

It took them two days to find their equipment in the scattered parachuted containers. At last, on Nov. 9, from their 4,000-foot mountain eyrie, in a tiny snow-covered hut, they made contact with Einar, who, a few miles away, was running a close race with the Gestapo.[3]

Operation "Gunnerside" went into action when six Norwegians were dropped onto the snow-covered ice of Lake Skryken, thirty miles north of the Swallows' hideout. It was the end of December. The men had to hole up for five desperate days in a blizzard, but finally they joined the Swallows. There were now eleven men, including Einar. He daily supplied the contingent with the latest details on the positions of the guards at the plant, the times that the guards changed, which gates were locked and how they were locked.

The final assault on the plant was a spine-tingling, drama-filled picture of courage and selflessness. After placing the explosives at strategic places inside the plant, the commandos made their way out before the big blow-up that sent 1,000 pounds of heavy water into the sewers.

Five of the six Gunnerside men later skied into Sweden and made their way safely back to England.

A sixth — Bonzo — and the four Swallows stayed behind to do underground work, playing tag with reinforced Nazi ski patrols. Einar retired to his cave-like lair to continue his watch on Norsk Hydro.[4]

Late in 1943, Einar reported that the plant had resumed operations. After American bombers knocked out the power station the Germans decided to move all of the heavy water equipment to an underground site in Germany.

Einar requested permission to sink the ferryboat *Hydro*, which was to take freight cars with the stocks of heavy water across Lake Tinnsjo. He and Bonzo placed time charges on the boat before she sailed. Hours later, the last of the deuterium oxide went to the bottom of the lake.

I put the magazine down on my bedside table. A profound gratitude flooded through me for the courage and dedication shown by Einar and his compatriots. I felt as if I'd been privileged to know — even to ski with and talk to — a human being of the calibre of Albert Schweitzer or Florence Nightingale . . . one who had helped save the western world from disaster.

By the end of April, the dismantling of the refinery was finished and the fitting together of pieces, like a jigsaw puzzle, was well under way in Edmonton. Einar came into the office to say "goodbye" to Eric, Les, Blatch, Win and me. He shook my hand and wished me well with my skiing.

Thirty-four years later, when doing research for this book, I found Einar's full name printed boldly in an Imperial Oil document. But to me, he'll always be just "Einar," a Second World War hero whose shadow briefly touched mine in the Yukon.

1. Frederic Sondern, Jr., "Eleven Against the Nazi A-Bomb," *The Reader's Digest*, November, 1946, The Reader's Digest Association (Canada) Ltd. Reprinted by special permission.
2. *Ibid.*
3. *Ibid.*
4. *Ibid.*

Chapter 24

The Donjek River was three miles wide, veering off into several channels in the area where the Alaska Highway crossed it. The original bridge, built by U.S. Army Engineers, was made up of seven wooden spans, each for a different channel.

The river is unpredictable. It flows from a source in the St. Elias range of mountains, where sits Mount Logan, 19,500 feet — highest mountain in Canada. The Donjek, at Mile 1,130, is only twenty miles south of Snag airbase, where the temperature in 1947 hit a record low of 82 degrees below zero (Fahrenheit). The ground is frozen year-round in the Donjek-Snag area.

In the spring, the river can look placid one hour, trickling quietly across the frozen channel beds, and the next hour it can look angry, tumbling in torrents from ice formations that are melting and moving in the mountains. Canadian engineers found it difficult to work on the new steel and concrete bridge because they never knew what the river would do in the spring. The existing wooden bridges, however, could not withstand the roaring spring run-offs any longer. Every year bridges had to be repaired, and often completely replaced.

Brigadier Walsh said, at a later date, that the U.S. Army had planned to put a steel bridge over the Donjek River. But, toward the end of the war, when the threat of a Japanese invasion was over, the steel was shipped across the Pacific for "the invasion of the Philippines."

After the war, Walsh stopped over in Manila on his way back from China. An engineer with the U..S. Public Roads Administration, a civilian consultant to the Army named Turner, took him to a U.S. Army bridging dump, "and pointed out to me the steel which was clearly marked for the Donjek Bridge."

Canadians re-designed the bridge, and Walsh explained this project as follows: "The original design for the bridge was a continuous steel structure, extremely long, but by re-design there was a considerable savings of steel."

In the spring of 1982, looking back on those early years of

Canadian Army involvement on the highway, Walsh pointed out that the permanent steel bridges built by the U.S. Army were set wrongly on their rockers. "Plans were designed for zero and not 80 below. We had to jack up all bridges the Americans had put in, and re-set them. The bridges were designed in Missouri."

* * *

Bridge work was top priority in those early days.

By April, 1948, No. 1 Road was well established at Mile 1,130, ready to begin driving pile for its third steel bridge — a bridge that would take four years to complete.

In June the Army built a cabin and furnished it so the wives of the men could take turns spending a few days at the camp. Georgina Keddell was the first wife to brave this Donjek wilderness.

"Pioneer living . . . but gorgeous country," she told me after her first visit.

In spite of working from dawn to dusk in the long daylight hours, Dan managed to come to town now and then. He began to grow on me. I loved to listen to the stories he told in his colorful narrative style — stories of the bridge and the road and the people who were making history. He spoke of big Hec MacDonald, a sergeant with No. 1 Road, whose quiet efficiency contrasted sharply with Jim Keddell's roar and nervous energy. Both men were about the same size — built like enormous polar bears. Then there was a big Swede named Nelson, who worked outside in 50-below-zero weather dressed in light trousers and a short-sleeved shirt. He swore he kept warm by belting down a couple of quarts of overproof rum each day.

That spring Dan gave me a gift   a mountain goat rug. He had shot the goat himself in the winter when he had first gone to the Donjek, and he had spent months tanning the hide and brushing the fur so it would look rich and warm on my bedroom floor.

Rena had been dating Roger Dowling, a private with Army Service Corps, and Betty had been seeing Wally Ellis. Roger, Wally and Dan often joined us for coffee and cards at the barrack. Our friends the Princess Pats had left in March, and we were back to normal living.

Al Hussey from the pay office sometimes wandered over with a book of Robert Service tucked under his arm. While we sewed or played cards, Al entertained us with recitations from Service:

So gaunt against the gibbous moon
Piercing the silence velvet-piled,
A lone wolf howls his ancient rune,
The fell arch-spirit of the Wild

One night, after an exciting evening of Service, Dan and I broke away from the group and went out for a quiet talk and coffee at the Klondyke. There, in a corner booth where a lone candle lighted the table, I told him about my dream of finding Million Dollar Valley.

"I've heard about that valley, but . . . I've also heard dozens of stories about the location. Northern British Columbia, Southern Yukon, Alaska."

Suddenly The Valley took on new dimensions. Where was it? "Surely somebody in the Air Force would know . . . somebody in an air crew?" I asked, feeling annoyed with myself for not getting the exact latitude and longitude from Brad. I'd just taken for granted that he knew the way, and I'd get there when I went with him. But now . . .

"This Yukon's a country of tall tales, of Million Dollar Valleys and Headless Valleys." Dan paused thoughtfully, then continued slowly. "You've got my interest, though. It would be exciting to see those bombers . . . if we could locate them."

I hadn't expected to share my dream with anyone, and yet, it seemed right to share it with Dan.

* * *

When the heat of summer descended on the Yukon that year, so did forest fires. The air in Whitehorse turned blue-gray and the sun was a dull crimson ball from dawn to dusk.

Keddell came to town and told us the fire was located in the Kluane Lake area, fifty miles south of the Donjek. Dan and half-a-dozen engineers from the camp were operating bulldozers night and day, trying to isolate the flames.

We felt as if we were living in a cocoon . . . the heavy, choking air always there, making our eyes smart and our throats sore. During the forest fire season we forgot our fear of a Russian invasion, forgot the transient nature of our existences. Our minds were preoccupied with the smoke and the possibility of having to evacuate in case the flames roared out of control.

The Kluane fire, however, was under control in a week. After this, the Destruction Bay camp, Mile 1083, held a Saturday night dance in the schoolhouse. Six of us hitched rides with a couple

Buildings at the Destruction Bay maintenance camp, Mile 1083, are pictured against a backdrop of mountains on the northern section of the Alaska Highway. This photograph was taken in 1946.
Photo by James Quong.

of soldiers driving Army weapons carriers from Whitehorse to the Donjek. We arrived about 10 p.m., when things were beginning to swing at Destruction. The men outnumbered the women ten to one, and all of the 100 soldiers and civilians from camps along the highway were there. Hip pockets bulged with bottles of hooch.

Johnny Friend, a Reemee worker at the auxiliary Reemee shop at Destruction, was there. Johnny, a tall, lean type, was well-known for his beard, which reached nearly to his bellybutton. Years later he said, "I was the Yukon's first hippie."

Back then he had to guard his beard carefully. He told us that if he got too drunk, there were people who would go wild with a razor and trim his handsome brush.

Flora MacDonald, big Hec's sister, who had the room next to mine in Forty-seven, was at the Destruction Bay party. Flora, a tall, dignified woman who had been a captain with the CWAC during the war, was the brigadier's secretary. She and I were avid readers, enjoying modern novels by Buck, Ferber, Remarque . . . poetry by Eliot, Pound. We often discussed books, and, in our

135

lighter moments, went down to the Regina Hotel in Whitehorse for an evening of ale.

At Destruction Bay, however, all dignity and books were forgotten as we jived, rumbaed, tangoed. Around midnight, Dan arrived. He told me that at the last dance he had attended in the schoolhouse, two young lieutenants, who had been feuding over a woman, had pulled guns on one another and fired at close range.

"Jaysus . . . we all ducked behind tables, chairs, you name it. Then these yokels began to laugh like nuts . . . standing in the middle of the floor. They had drawn blanks."

There wasn't any such excitement that night, but a few fights broke out, and we heard later that a number of soldiers didn't make it back to Whitehorse for church parade the next day.

We danced all night and had breakfast at the small camp mess hall the next morning. After this, Dan drove us ten miles north where we went to Mass at the Burwash Landing mission church, set in a picturesque spot on the shore of Kluane Lake. Here the air still reeked of stale smoke, and we saw how the fire had leveled miles of land on the other side of the highway. I remembered the fireweed, and knew that in the autumn this purple flower would fling its mantle high to cover the devastation.

Chapter 25

Rena Fraser was married that summer of '48. It was a simple ceremony in the old log church in Whitehorse — built in 1900. Dan and I were attendants, and the bride, who was seldom on time for a rendezvous, was fifteen minutes late for her wedding.

Bridegroom Roger Dowling was a calm, easy-going lad who accepted this "lateness" in his stride, but Dan was nervous.

"I didn't think you two women would ever get there. We stood at the altar for *hours,* and I kept thinking that nothing could be worse than to be stood up at your own wedding," Dan said, as we four sat down to a post-wedding dinner in the dining room of the inn.

Rena had told me two months before the big date that she and Roger would be married. She wanted a quiet wedding, however, with just the four of us in the church. We guarded the secret carefully, but in spite of this Blatch found out.

"I hear Rena's getting married," he told me one day, and when I denied knowing anything about it, he laughed. "This is a strange road, this Alaska Highway . . . linked together by Army camps . . . one big family. I know what people in Dawson Creek are thinking five minutes after they think it."

He was right. News travelled with missilelike swiftness along the road. We knew all the camps from Mile 0 to the Alaska border, and distances were dissolved in seconds by phone, telegraph or mental telepathy. Therefore, I wasn't surprised a few weeks later when Blatch told me he'd heard that *I* was going to be married.

I wasn't sure when it happened . . . when I knew I was in love with the Glengarry Scot who could tell a story punctuated with more colorful anecdotes than I could ever put on paper. I only knew it was a sudden, forceful thing that I hadn't planned on when I'd left Edmonton to see the Far North. Dan was an adventurer who loved the bush and the road and the solitude of the great back-of-beyond. I knew that, as a writer, I would have to write about life as it flowed around me, and he would eventually emerge, a whole or fragmented picture on the page. I also knew that I would have to have solitude, too . . . to think and put pen to paper, and freedom to paint any picture I desired.

We talked at great length about our needs, hopes, desires; they were diverse in many respects, but we had a lot in common, too . . . the same family backgrounds, religious faith, love of the outdoors. We liked to read, too . . . histories, novels, poetry.

* * *

Roger Dowling was transferred to Fort St. John, and Rena followed him there shortly afterwards. She was hired by Ma Murray to help launch the paper each week. The barrack was quiet without Rena's effervescent footsteps and hearty laugh.

One night as Betty, Tudy and I ate a late-night snack in the reception room, Win Haines came flying down the hall.

"I caught him . . . caught him," she cried, leaping through the reception room and out the door. We looked at one another in startled amazement.

"What's she talking about?" asked Tudy.

"Who knows?" commented Betty. We went back to our snack, then Win came flying in out of the cool night.

"I almost caught him, you dopes. I screamed at you to come and help."

"Caught who?" we echoed.

"The peeper."

"What?"

She ran to the phone and dialed the RCMP (Mounties). When she returned, she sank down into an easy chair, and, still out of breath from her run, told us that earlier, as she'd combed her hair in the washroom, she had seen the peeper's profile sliding across the open window now and then. She inched her way over to the outside wall. The next time his cap appeared she reached out and grabbed him by the collar. She struggled to get a good look at his face. He thrashed around wildly to get away. She called for help. We didn't hear. It was pitch dark outside. The lights from the washroom spilled out the window. Win — who was wiry and strong — yanked the intruder into the light. He hid his face in his coat. He kicked . . . flailed. The window was high. She tried to haul him through. He braced his feet against the side of the building and broke her hold. She ran down the hall and outside where she chased him half a block. He got away.

Later that night the RCMP phoned Win to tell her they had apprehended someone. We never found out his identity, but he must have been the right person, because from then on our peeper problems vanished.

Chapter 26

The women who worked for the Northwest Highway System in those early days were adventurers. There was a bold fearlessness about them. They were conscientious workers on the job. They kept telephone lines operating day and night, Army accounts balanced, hospital records straight, all-important communication channels open between Whitehorse and Ottawa . . . Whitehorse and Edmonton. (One woman — Dorothy Miller — drove a diesel truck full-time up and down the highway.) And after work, these women climbed mountains, hitchhiked the length of the road, canoed down rivers, skied across valleys.

In 1946 the three Canadian women's services — Army (CWAC), Navy (WRCNS) and Air Force RCAF (W.D.) — were disbanded. In 1951, the cabinet approved the enrollment of women in the militia to a maximum of 8,850. Many women workers on the NWHS had been in one of the services during the war, but had been discharged by 1946 and served as civilians on the highway. Others, like me, had never been in the armed forces, but there was this common bond between us: a desire for adventure, a need to see the other side of the mountain.

* * *

We were all fascinated with the Ace Away game. As we walked east on Main Street past the big old-fashioned theatre building and turned the corner onto Third Avenue, there was an innocent sign — Yukon Sportsman's Club — which disguised the gambling den. As patrons opened the door to go in, we saw cement steps descending into the bowels of the theatre. Although gambling was illegal under the criminal code of Canada, the RCMP ignored the little den and its sign. There was a brassy ring of Dawson City before the turn of the century as hobnailed boots and mukluks beat a path into this dimly lit, hazy underworld.

Soldiers and airmen often spent all their pay cheques, watched the crumpled green lettuce pile up on the table, eyed with anticipation the dealer as he tossed three dice from a rubber cup and called out, "Jing-a-low for all that dough."

The Ace Away game was closed by the RCMP in 1950, ending a colorful era of gambling in the Yukon.

I was sitting in the Klondyke having a coffee one Saturday morning in the summer of '48 when a guy sitting next to me started to talk. He was a dealer, and he told me it was not uncommon for $50,000 to pile up on the Ace Away table in a night.

"I've always wanted to go and see the big dice roll. I suppose people can just watch?" I asked.

He shook his head. "Women can't go. They're bad luck."

"What?" I exclaimed, feeling as if I'd suddenly sprouted horns. "Do you *throw* them out if they go?"

He was a short, bald man with beady eyes. He squirmed uneasily in his chair. "No. If a woman appears, the play stops."

Flora MacDonald decided she would call his bluff. On a dark moonless night, she and her boyfriend walked over to the club and descended the steps into the inner sanctum. She watched while the dice rolled once . . . twice . . . then somebody spotted her, and, as though a streak of lightning had hit, everybody froze. She didn't think there was much sense in arguing. She left quietly.

By the time we women mobilized to fight, collectively, this discrimination . . . the game was outlawed.

Although we didn't get a chance to gamble at the Ace Away, we gambled in other ways . . . and, not always with money . . . sometimes with our lives.

* * *

I was called to the phone at the mess hall on a warm July evening. The male voice introduced himself.

"Bob Smith . . . Air Force, Hope. We're revving up a Dak to go to Watson Lake for a party. The C.O. there is going out on posting. Would you like to come along?"

Watson Lake was about 300 miles south of Whitehorse.

"What time are you leaving?"

"Seven."

I looked at my watch. It was six-thirty. This last-minute invitation didn't give me much time to change clothes and get up to the air base.

"I'm one of the pilots. We'd sure like to have you come along . . . and any of the other Army girls, too. It'll be a good party."

140

There were about eight stragglers finishing dinner in the mess hall. It was a Friday night. We worked Saturdy morning, but that didn't deter us from hurrying home, changing into party dresses and rushing, in a cab, up to the air base.

The Dak crew was in the Yukon to photograph the territory for maps. The men had done only two weeks of a three-month stint. Their permanent base was Ottawa.

After we were airborne I had a strange, uneasy feeling about the trip. I knew that booze would flow like ouzo at a Greek wedding. I wondered what would happen if all four pilots got drunk. Also, it seemed to me that if they had just come from Ottawa, they wouldn't be very familiar with this rugged terrain.

Half an hour after take-off, Bob Smith sauntered through the door of the cockpit, walked along the aisle and sat down beside me.

"I knew Tim Condon. A guy at the base in Whitehorse told me you were a friend of Tim's."

"Yes. He was a great guy."

"Good pilot . . . but, when your number's up, it's up."

"Yeah." I sighed, remembering. "Life isn't always fair, is it?"

"No."

The uneasy feeling escalated to a nagging worry. I decided to spell it out. "Will you and the other pilots be drinking at the party?"

He smiled broadly. "Don't you know that there are old pilots and bold pilots, but there are no old bold pilots?"

He left to return to the cockpit, but his conscience must have bothered him, because he came back later, sat beside me and said, "There's always one pilot who doesn't drink when we go to a party, and tonight that one is me."

I felt more reassured, and because he seemed to want to talk, and because Million Dollar Valley had been on my mind all day, I asked him if he had heard of the mysterious last resting place for the three B-26 bombers, the Marauders.

"No," he said, shaking his head quizzically. "You mean four B-26s crashed in this remote spot?"

"They were following the leader and the leader got lost."

"Wow."

"I have great hopes of seeing that valley someday. Actually, Tim Condon was the first person to tell me about it. Tim was fascinated with The Valley."

"Really?" He stroked his chin thoughtfully. "I must find out more about it. It's really hard to believe, isn't it . . . that bombers that big could land intact."

141

"One after the other."

A bright moon cast a sheen across the waters of Watson Lake as we landed. The barrack building and quonset huts were similar to those in Whitehorse. I felt at home, and yet, I was wishing we'd come in the daylight when I might have looked around. The ghost of Tim Condon seemed to linger there. We were ushered into the officers' mess, where sandwiches and coffee awaited us.

"We heard that you people hadn't had time for supper, so we phoned ahead and asked for the food," said Bob.

On the highly polished spruce walls of the mess, American and Canadian officers had written or carved their names. I searched the various scrawled signatures and found Tim Condon there in bold, indelible pen. I could almost hear him, as though his voice was echoing across miles, "Look, kid . . . don't forget The Valley."

After we'd finished our sandwiches and coffee, we went to a nearby hangar that was decorated with swaying streamers and balloons in psychedelic colors. A small orchestra played up a storm, and we danced until three o'clock in the morning. Then we helped ourselves to a smorgasbord dinner of moose steak with all the trimmings. A silver tray was presented to the C.O. and his wife. There were speeches. We sang "Will ye no come back again."

The Dak trembled as it revved at the end of the runway. Suddenly we were in the air, going home.

Bob invited me into the cockpit to see the sun coming up. The curved plexiglass windshields afforded a panoramic view of the mountains silhouetted against the brilliant coral canvas of the rising sun.

"Visibility's good," he said, manipulating levers.

Everything had gone well and everybody'd had a good time, but the nagging uneasiness was still there like a lead weight. I couldn't seem to shake off the heavy feeling it created. I returned to my seat, took a book that I'd tossed in for reading on the airplane out of my purse. Everybody — including members of the orchestra, with their instruments beside them — slept. The hum of the engine was soothing. I could see the sun, now golden, through the small window at my side. One of the pilots marched down the aisle and told us to fasten our seat belts. I stuffed my book into my purse because I knew we'd be landing in about ten minutes. Thirty minutes later we still had not landed, and I sensed there was something wrong. I undid my belt and went into the cockpit. Outside, a dense fog clung to the windshield like sticky cotton candy.

"Are you having trouble?" I asked the co-pilot.

142

" Yeah. We can't seem to contact the GCA boys at Whitehorse."

GCA meant "ground control approach." Without this ground contact, a plane could not come in on instruments, and I knew that an instrument landing was the only way to go in a fog like the one I could see through the window.

"Where are the GCA boys?" I gulped.

"I dunno. We've radioed Edmonton and they told us to go up to another level and wait for a break in the clouds."

"But . . . what about the emergency flight strip between Watson and Whitehorse?"

"It's fogged in . . . and so is Watson."

Bob, at the controls, was worried. "Look, Hope, go back to your seat."

I hurried back. My friends and members of the orchestra were still curled up, asleep. Some of them were snoring. Oblivion. Sweet oblivion. I was jealous.

I was alert to the tiniest noise, fragments of my imagination flying here and there on greased wings. What would it be like to crash? In those hairbrush forests and wild mountains, we'd never be found. I looked out my porthole window and saw only solid wool. Gawd! Nobody in Whitehorse knew we'd even left. We hadn't had time to leave a note. There wasn't a passenger list for the plane, either. Although the C.O. at the Whitehorse base had given permission for the trip, it had been an unscheduled flight.

Another fifteen minutes went by as we searched for a break in the clouds. It looked hopeless. I wondered how much gas we had, but I didn't dare ask. I likened us to a ghost ship riding the dizzy circle of a Sargasso Sea, hoping for rescue. Then I saw it . . . a single ray of sunlight penetrating the cotton wool. The ship turned in a half circle. We went straight down through that narrow slit. The clouds moved to let us through. It was a strange feeling . . . the clouds swirling around us, the sun penetrating the moving mists like shooting rainbows.

The airfield was swathed in a shifting mist as we set our wheels down.

"Let's go for coffee," Bob said, as he caught up with me before I stepped into a waiting cab.

In the Whitehorse Inn, hunched over our coffee mugs, he murmured, "That was a close call. We were almost out of gas. I haven't felt that scared since I flew bombers overseas."

"Mom wants to know if it's an all-cement highway"

Harold Hubbard's gifted pen lightened the workload for the U.S. Army and the Canadian Army forces working along the Alaska Highway, made the bitter winters a little warmer, and helped tempers dissolve into chuckles. Hubbard, stationed in the Yukon and the Northwest Territories with the U.S. Army Signal Corps from 1942 to 1945, is now retired and living in Lansing, Michigan.

This cartoon was taken from Harold Hubbard's book of cartoons, titled Arctic Issue, lithographed by the Hamly Press, Ltd., Edmonton, Alberta, 1945.

Chapter 27

In the evenings, that summer of '48, we played softball in the ballpark where a big post office building stands today. In the early part of July, we played a final game at midnight one night, the sun hovering like a harvest moon on the horizon. Someone belted a ball out to centre field, and an outfielder actually caught it.

One Friday evening, after an earlier game, Dan called to me from the bleachers and came running down to the field where I stood with several players.

"I've got a vehicle. Let's go out to the lodge at Marsh Lake . . . have a drink."

I felt dusty and sweaty after playing ball, but it didn't matter. I hadn't seen Dan for a month.

He was driving an Army weapons carrier that was open to the mountain winds. It was a mellow evening with the sun slanting across the world in a hazy glow. There was no traffic. The breeze we created, as we flew down the highway, gently tossed our hair. Thirty miles away, Dan stopped at a picturesque lodge that overlooked Marsh Lake. We sat near one of the large windows in the lounge and ordered martinis.

"I've got a gift for you," he said. "It's something you've wanted for a long time."

He reached inside the tunic of his uniform and drew out a dark-green, hard-cover book.

"*Arctic Issue*," I exclaimed excitedly, recognizing the book of cartoons that I loved so well. "Where the heck did you get a copy?"

"Would you believe . . . they're so scarce now you have to buy them on the black market."

By the light of a flickering candle on the table, and the pale rays of the sun filtering through the window, we studied again the cartoons penned by Harold Hubbard, a sergeant who had served with the U.S. Army Signal Corps on the Alaska Highway and the CANOL pipeline.

I had been introduced to this book more than a year before when

I'd first arrived in Whitehorse. Betty had shown me her copy one evening in old Seventeen, and we had roared at the graphic, humorous pictures Hubbard had created of the Army in the Far North.

Three thousand copies of the book had been printed in 1945 by Hamly Press, Edmonton. It had been approved for publication by Maj. Freeman C. Bishop, of the Public Relations Branch, Headquarters, Northwest Service Command, U.S. Army.

By the time the Canadian Army arrived in April, 1946, all books had been sold. However, there were enough personal copies floating around in camps up and down the highway to give Canadian soldiers and civilians some hearty chuckles. Dan knew that I wanted a copy of the book for my own, and now, with book copy in hand, we turned the pages slowly. Two oversized characters leaped out at us. Both were dressed in sloppy parkas and boots as they faced one another. The caption hit home: "Don't you recognize an officer when you see one?"

We turned the pages again and paused. Three parka-clad guys with jutting chins faced another three with the same mean chins. Between these stubborn factions, two ends of a pipeline were a long way from connecting with one another. The caption said, "MACMILLAN PASS — east and west pipelines will meet here 16 February 1944."

We turned the pages again and paused at another picture of a dump truck overturned on the highway, a private in gum boots trying to jockey the outfit upright with a stick. Beyond this, on a curved stretch of road, another outfit was mired down in gumbo mud. A road sign said, "MUNCHO LAKE." A corporal sat on a stone beside the road, reading a letter, and the caption was, "Mom wants to know if it's an all cement highway?"

We read an introduction in the book, dated February 20, 1944: "The question has been raised recently whether there is anything funny about a war, and we've concluded that the general reputation of Army humor is based on myth. If so, the myth seems to us to be pretty active again. In what is surely the most destructive, horror-ridden war in history, a war so bad that it causes even the most optimistic to gravely question the fundamental goodness of human nature, there is the wonderful paradox that it is also a war of shining humor, of Sad Sack and Bob Hope, of Mauldin and Private Hargrove."

I tucked *Arctic Issue* carefully into my purse with a special "thank you," and Dan and I talked again about getting married. We had decided that we would go ahead and take the big step, but we wanted to do it quietly, as Rena had done.

"It's impossible to get married quietly in Whitehorse," Dan said. "We know too many people. Word would get out. Rena was lucky."

"Where do you suggest?"

"The little log church at Kluane Lake. I go there an odd Sunday for Mass. It's only about fifty miles from the Donjek."

"But it's nearly two hundred miles from Whitehorse . . . and the buses aren't very dependable," I reminded him.

"That's a small problem. I can take care of it."

"How?"

"It's a secret."

Secrets always interested me, but I knew that I would have to let that one go, for now. I remembered the church from my only visit there the weekend a group of us had gone to the party at Destruction Bay. Rustic baskets of wild flowers had hung from the ceiling, near the altar. Wide, scuffed floorboards and rough pews were reminiscent of an earlier era.

The church seemed like a perfect place for a quiet wedding; the lake, flanked by high mountains, was the perfect setting for a honeymoon.

"Gene Jacquot has just finished building a two-storey log hotel at Burwash. Also . . . he has cabins on the lake that he rents for fifty dollars a month. I'll try to get one for a month."

Jacquot was a pioneer who had built an empire at Burwash Landing, a settlement on the shore of Kluane.

My mind flew into high gear. "A week is all the time I can get. I've already had my vacation."

"Okay. I'll arrange everything."

"Late August or early September."

"Right."

The sun kissed the horizon in a passionate burst of fuschia, then began to rise again. A heavy dew had settled across the world. As we drove back to Whitehorse, the dew glistened on the leaves of the small poplars that lined the road, and it clung to the windshield of the old weapons carrier like a fine rain.

Chapter 28

In mid-August I received a letter from my dad.

"Monsignor O'Gorman phoned today to tell me you've asked for your baptism certificate, and I assume you're getting married. I hope you've carefully considered this step in your life. Nowadays, it's more difficult to untie that knot than it is to tie it. I've always maintained that marriage laws should be made tougher rather than divorce laws more lenient. I've never met Dan, and I guess I'm behaving like an old mother hen."

I felt sad when I read the letter. Dan and I decided that, because of the distances involved in travelling to Kluane, we wouldn't tell our relatives about our plans until the wedding was over. I sensed my dad felt hurt because he had to learn about my marriage through a telephone call from a parish priest. I phoned him and we had a quiet talk. I couldn't explain too much about the upcoming wedding because I did not know what arrangements Dan was making. My father understood.

Later, Dan sent me a letter which told me he had arranged for our wedding on Saturday, September 4, at eight o'clock at night. However, by Friday, transportation arrangements still had not been finalized. I worked on Friday until five o'clock in the afternoon. Dan phoned from the Donjek that night.

"Look . . . Freddy Haines left this afternoon for Whitehorse. See if you can talk him into coming back tomorrow. I'll meet you at three o'clock in the afternoon at Haines Junction."

"Okay. If I can't get Freddy to go back . . . I'll phone you."

"Good."

Fred was Win's brother. He was in charge of the auxiliary Reemee shop at Destruction Bay. I flew down the hall to Win's room.

"I need your help," I told her.

"What's up?"

"I'm getting married tomorrow, and —"

"What? Jeez . . . really?"

"Really. Burwash Landing . . . tomorrow night . . . only I have no way of getting there."

A rustic log cabin on the shore of Lake Kluane was the honeymoon home of Hope Morritt and Dan Cameron following their wedding in the mission church at Burwash Landing.

This portion of the Alaska Highway follows Kluane Lake — the largest lake in the Yukon, with 153 square miles of water. Hope and Dan took this route in an Army dump truck before their marriage at the mission at Burwash Landing on the shore of the lake. At this particular site near Soldier's Summit a special ceremony was held in November, 1943 by the U.S. Army to mark the completion of the tote road from Dawson Creek, B.C., to Fairbanks, Alaska.

Photo by James Quong.

"You sure kept quiet about it. But look . . . Fred's in town. He'll take you . . . us, I mean. Jeez . . . it's exciting. Let's go find Fred."

My "surprise" transportation was an Army pickup truck with Win, Fred and me crammed into the front seat, a small suitcase jammed with wedding array at my feet. Fred stopped every twenty or thirty miles to take a swig of Johnny Walker, and Win and I got annoyed with him.

"C'mon. We want t' get there in one piece, Fred."

"Ah . . . just a little one . . . for the bride."

"Smarten up. I don't need 'a little one'."

"Okay."

A tall, lean man with a warm, friendly smile, Fred was easy-going, which was lucky for us.

Win and I had worked side by side for more than a year. We had shared jokes, shopping sprees, meals, personal triumphs and tragedies. I loved her droll sense of humor. She dated a handsome RCMP constable named Bill Thurber, and later she married him. It was good to share with Win and Fred these exciting moments prior to my wedding.

Dan was waiting at Haines Junction, 98 miles northwest of Whitehorse — a small settlement where the road to Haines, Alaska, veered off in one direction, and the Alaska Highway continued in the other. I climbed out of the pickup.

"See you at Burwash," hollered Win.

With those words ringing in my ears, I climbed into my wedding car — a brand-new Army dump truck.

Dan and I laughed as we jaunted along. We were on wheels. We didn't care what kind of wheels.

"I've got the jalopy for a week. They might come and get it if they need it, but . . . what the hell." He shrugged as though that didn't matter. "One day we'll own a Caddy and we'll come back in style."

Those words were prophetic. Twenty-nine years later we came back for a visit . . . in a Caddy. But back then, sailing along in the Army truck, the here and now pressed in gently upon us. The mountain peaks were bathed in mists and the lowlands were brilliant with autumn colors of crimson and gold. The world was peaceful, the curtain of twilight slowly descending.

***

Dan had rented a log cabin on the shore of the lake. Sparsely furnished, the cabin had two bedrooms and a large kitchen-living room with a big wood-burning kitchen range that supplied heat.

Georgina and Jim greeted us when we arrived at the cabin. They'd been there about an hour, having driven down from the Donjek to be witnesses at our wedding.

The night settled in . . . black, cool and clear. At 7:45 p.m., Jim, Georgina, Dan and I walked along a crooked trail to the church about 500 feet away. The stars were so bright it looked as if somebody had taken a handful of sequins and flung them at the black dome of heaven.

The little church was lit up, its small windows like bright beacons in the night. But . . . if we thought we had planned a quiet wedding, we were in for a shock. The church was full, Indians from the nearby settlement filling one side, and soldiers from the Donjek and Destruction Bay camps filling the other. Wildflowers decorated the altar. Mingled with the smell of incense was the pungent odor of buckskin.

Dan looked handsome in his Army uniform, the buttons and insignia resplendent from an extra application of elbow grease. He had had his handlebar moustache and hair trimmed, washed and brushed, and his usual rugged aura had been replaced with a certain polish. Jim, too, was in uniform, and, in spite of his bigness, he looked trim and smart.

I wore a simple aqua wool suit with white accessories.

Father Eurebe Morrisette, on oblate missionary, officiated, and later, while we signed the register, the priest told us he would visit us at our cabin sometime during the week.

Friends ushered us over to the nearby cafe, where Mary and Harvey, who operated the diner for Gene Jacquot, had set a big table with a wedding feast.

Georgina, always the writer, took her notebook out of her purse. "This is all so romantic, exciting. I'll do a story on you two for the *Star*. I'm absolutely fascinated with that ring." She took my hand to study in more detail the gold nugget ring Dan had given me for a wedding band.

"It's called a sluice box ring . . . made to resemble the old sluice boxes that miners used, years ago, for washing gravel to claim gold," I told her.

"Sluice box!" she exclaimed. "I don't like that."

"But . . . that's what the ring's called."

"It's not very romantic," she insisted.

I smiled when I read in the *Whitehorse Star* the following week: "The bride's ring was a wide band studded with gold nuggets, a replica of that other era of romantic yesterdays when gold was king in the Yukon."

We drank, ate, talked, sang, laughed and danced . . . to music supplied by an old jukebox. The hours slid away, unnoticed, like mercury through fingers.

Just before an old mantle clock above an open fireplace struck three, Jim rose, lifted high a glass of overproof rum and said, "To the bride." Impromptu speeches followed in noisy succession, then somebody broke into song, with the wedding guests joining in to give us a hearty send-off:

> There's a husky-dusky maiden in the Arctic
> In her igloo she is waiting there in vain
> And some day I'll put my mukluks on and ask her
> If she'll wed me when the ice worms nest again.
>
> In the land of pale blue snow
> Where it's ninety-nine below
> And the polar bears are roamin' o'er the plain
> In the shadow of the Pole
> I will clasp her to my soul
> We'll be happy when the ice worms nest again."

On that chorus, we newlyweds left to walk the short distance to our first home.

Newlyweds Hope Morritt and Dan Cameron stand in front of the Kluane Inn on the shore of Kluane Lake, Yukon. They spent a week in a cabin near the Inn following their wedding at the nearby mission church.

Chapter 29

On Monday morning Dan and I went over to the office in the hotel. Everything smelled of new lumber, varnish, and linoleum. The bulky-looking building, which had opened for business the week before, had one guest — a tourist from Montana. We used washroom facilities in the hotel and hauled water each day to our cabin next-door, but, on this Monday morning, we came over to use the phone. I talked at length to my dad in Edmonton, and across the humming wires I introduced him to Dan. There were tears and laughter as pictures of my wedding day spilled across the miles. An hour later there was an encore when we phoned Cornwall and talked to Dan's mother, Eva Cameron.

Late in the day, I called the Reemee office in Whitehorse to talk to Blatchford, but Les told me the major was still "out of town." I had tried to locate Blatch on my last day at work. Although I had phoned all his old haunts from Dawson Creek to Whitehorse, nobody had seen him. I phoned his home, but neither his wife nor his teen-age daughter, Averil, were home. I felt sad that I'd been unable to let him know about my marriage. I told Les on the phone that I would be back at work in a week, and he said that would be OK.

With all the telephone formalities behind us, Dan and I began to explore the colorful history of Burwash Landing. We learned the settlement was named after Locky Burwash, a Dominion government surveyor who settled there in 1901. Kluane Lake, 153 square miles of water, was the largest lake in the Yukon, and Burwash was located at the north end, half a mile off the Alaska Highway.

Four years after gold was discovered in the Klondike, lone prospectors working the creeks that flowed into Kluane hit pay dirt. Ten cents to the pan was a big find in those days, and word spread quickly that miners were making that and much more near Kluane. A stampede followed, and in 1904 Gene Jacquot and his brother, Louis, who had been lured to Dawson from France in 1898, made their way to the site of the new stampede.

They opened a trading post and called the village that sprang up around it Burwash Landing, after Locky Burwash. Athapascan Indians had lived here, in brush tents, for centuries. They had hunted and fished around the lake. These Indians called themselves "stick" Indians, people who live in the Interior among the trees.

Although the stampede for gold lasted little more than a year, the Jacquot brothers stayed. Gene, thirty-two at that time, was a sharp entrepreneur who saw a future in big-game hunting. He evolved, through the years, into the Yukon's most famous big-game guide.

In September, 1948, when we met him, he was seventy-six. A stocky man with sparse gray hair, he was nonetheless a rugged-looking, rather handsome man. His sons had taken over the big-game business, and he often could be seen in his office at the back of a shed, where he conducted business from behind a big desk.

Gene kept his packhorses in a corral on the other side of the highway. One afternoon when the sun was shining with an Indian summer brilliance, Dan and I decided to go horseback riding. We approached Gene in his office.

"We'd like to rent a couple of your horses . . . go for a ride," Dan said.

"You know where the horses are? In the corral?" He took his glasses off and studied us through astute, squinting eyes.

Dan nodded.

"Well . . . you'll have to catch them."

"No problem. My dad and I used to break horses, sell them . . . back in Ontario."

Gene grinned. "Then you won't have any trouble. Take your pick. Come back to the barn for saddles. No charge."

"But . . ." Dan began to protest the "no charge."

Gene cut him off. "No charge. Just go." With those words he impatiently dismissed us.

There were about thirty horses grazing in the big meadow. Dan positioned himself on a small knoll, and when a sleek brown mare came close, he jumped on her back. The antics that followed would have made a circus performer envious. The mare kicked up her hind legs. When Dan hung on, she reared up on her front legs. Still . . . he hung on. She followed with a tricky buck from the rear. Dan went flying, doing a somersault in midair. Standing nearby, on another hill, with a rope and halter in hand, I thought I was going to be an early widow. Dan made a graceful landing, though, in a patch of wild grass that cushioned his fall. We learned later that the mare had never been broken.

Pioneer Bert Cluett, left, bartender at Burwash Landing, chats with Staff Sgt. Fred Haines. This picture was taken after he trimmed his belly-length beard.

After that near-disaster we tried again, and caught two mares that were spirited but easy for us to manage. We rode them back to Jacquot's barn in the settlement, saddled them and took them through a maze of beautiful trails around the lake. Each afternoon we went horseback riding, enjoying the crisp air and the autumn colors. We did not see Gene again, but we often saw his Indian wife, Ruth (nicknamed "Pete") driving around in a new

Cadillac. She was years younger than Gene . . . a friendly, big woman with a warm smile.

Louis had died the year before. Between them, the two brothers and their Indian wives had eight children — six boys and two girls. The children went out, year after year, to Vancouver and France for an education. One of Louis's daughters recalled that, in the 1930s, she, along with her brother, sister and cousins, were driven to Whitehorse by wagon each autumn. It took nearly a week to cover the 186 miles on the rough wagon road. From Whitehorse the children flew out to Vancouver, and Louis's son, Louis, Jr., went on to France. At a later date, the Alaska Highway followed the route of the primitive wagon road of the 1930s.

Father Morrisette visited us one evening, and we soon learned that there had been uneasy moments between him and the Jacquots. Both brothers had slipped away from "the faith," and when Louis died the priest refused to bury him. The Roman Catholic bishop of the Yukon intervened, however, giving the priest permission to bury Louis with all the rites of the church.

Gene died that winter of 1948, after forty-four years as king of a wilderness realm. The brothers are buried side by side, in a cemetery near the settlement.

An old-timer named Bert Cluett, who was seventy-three in 1948, tended bar and waited on tables in the beer parlor owned by Gene. Bert was a short, frail man with a gray, bushy beard that reached nearly to his bellybutton. He shuffled back and forth in his deerskin moccasins, always dressed in the same baggy pants and plaid shirt. Although he was a man of few words, he liked to talk of the old days. He had come to Kluane in 1903 to seek a fortune. The gold fever had died quickly, when it was found the streams yielded less than five cents to the pan, but Bert stayed and helped the Jacquot brothers with their various ventures. Dan and I went over each evening for a brew, just to hear Bert talk.

"Don't stay in the Yukon longer 'n two years. If ye do, an' leave, ye'll always be scratchin' t' come back," he told us.

Bert was one who had stayed "too long." He went out to Vancouver many times and worked at odd jobs, only to come hurrying back to Burwash. He outlived the Jacquot brothers by twenty-three years, finally departing this life in 1971 at ninety-six. He is buried in the cemetery near the settlement.

Paddy and Jock (an Irishman and a Scot), civilians working as laborers at the Donjek, visited us at our cabin the day before we left Burwash. Meticulously dressed in tweed suits, white shirts, ties and highly polished shoes, they seemed different from the ordinary adventurers in the North. In the first place, their English was beautiful to hear, rolling off their lips in musical cadences. There were no errors in grammar, no twangy slang terms. I was surprised when they spoke, with great feeling, of the poetry of their native lands. Jock, with just the right touch of drama, recited Bobby Burns and gave us a small sample of English poetry with renditions of Byron, Keats and Shelley. Paddy loved Yeats and Padraic Pearse, the Irish rebel schoolteacher who was executed by the English. With great feeling he recited Pearse's famous poem, *The Mother.*

If I had been to a Shaw performance at Massey Hall in Toronto, I could not have been more impressed and excited.

"What wonderful guys," I told Dan after Paddy and Jock had bowed out of the cabin and driven off.

"Believe it or not, but they're university grads — metallurgists — and they *can* be gentlemen," said Dan.

"Can?" I echoed.

"Yes, when they lay off the booze. A month ago, at three o'clock in the morning, one of the civilians woke me. 'You'll have t' do something with Jock and Paddy. Christ! They're so rowdy we can't sleep,' he said."

"Rowdy? Those two gentlemen?"

Dan nodded. "I got dressed that night, walked the five hundred feet over to the other barrack, and paused in the hallway outside their door."

"They share a room?"

"Yeah . . . cots, in a single room. Cardboard-thin walls. Paddy'd passed out on a bunk, and Jock, seated on the other bunk, nursed an empty bottle of rum. 'I'm gonna cut off your head,' he shouted. 'I'm gonna cut it off and put it into a gunny sack . . . and I'm gonna bury it . . . and you'll never find it again, you won't. You'll never find it."

Dan shook his head sadly. "I didn't laugh till the next day, because when Paddy and Jock are drunk, each one is capable of cutting off the other's head, and . . . who'd find it in this back-of-beyond?"

The next day I got a ride to Whitehorse with Jim and Georgina, and Dan and the dump truck went the other way . . . back to bridge-building at the Donjek.

Chapter 30

Major Blatchford was at his desk when I arrived early for work on Monday morning. Through the glass partition that divided the offices I could see that he was immersed in paperwork, his desk lamp throwing a warm glow around the room. I knocked at his door, and he grumbled, "Come in."

Although there was a hum of activity in the workshop beyond the thick cement wall, we were alone in the offices. With trepidation, I began, "Sorry I couldn't get word to you about my wedding, Major. I —"

He cut me off with a dark look. "I really like to be informed well ahead of time when one of my staff takes off for a week's leave, Miss Morritt."

The air was thick with bad vibrations, but I decided to hold my ground. "I didn't know the exact date of my wedding until the day before —"

"A day would have given me time to consider a leave."

"But . . . I couldn't locate you, Major Blatchford. I phoned up and down the road from Dawson to Whitehorse, with no success in finding you."

He dismissed my words with a wave of his hand and explained it wasn't *that* difficult to locate people on the Northwest Highway System.

For the sake of honesty, I decided to take a chance on incurring his wrath and perhaps losing my job. "But . . . it's often very difficult if not *impossible* at times, to locate *you.*"

He looked down at his paperwork, and suddenly I felt sorry for him. He seemed rather sad, perhaps ill . . . certainly not his old exuberant self. In a week's time he would jokingly tell his staff he had been "boozing" too much, and that he had turned over a new leaf; he had climbed aboard the water wagon. Now, however, he looked rather shaky, old; and yet I knew he was only forty-one. He heaved a long ragged sigh and looked at me again.

"Miss Morritt, there's a lot of work here. You could get started on this month-end activity report I've put together in the rough."

158

He handed me a sheaf of papers. Until we parted several months later, Blatchford never acknowledged my marriage. I remained on the Army payroll under my own name — Hope Morritt — and he always referred to me by that name.

* * *

On weekends I was busy looking for a small house that Dan and I could rent until our names surfaced for an Army apartment. Couples with children were given priority for occupancy of new apartment complexes the Army was building on the hill. This left us at the bottom of the list.

After searching for a couple of weeks I rented a three-room furnished house in Whiskey Flats. Our rent was $50 a month. We paid for the electricity separately, and we hauled our water in galvanized pails from the river, a stone's throw away.

Chopping wood for the ever-hungry kitchen range kept us busy. The weather was beginning to get colder, and because we could buy only softwood — spruce or poplar — which burned like cardboard, our fuel supplies quickly dwindled. The kitchen stove was used for heating as well as cooking. We had to set the alarm at two-hour intervals during the night, an alert to feed the stove so we could rise in a warm place and cook breakfast. In the daytime we came home to a cold hearth and spent an hour coaxing the fire so we could warm up enough to make supper. Neither Dan nor I liked this pioneer approach to life, but we knew it would be a temporary arrangement only.

I walked by Brad's old house on the way to work. New owners had completely renovated the place, and it looked so different with its gable ends and white picket fence that I barely recognized it. Nevertheless, it triggered a few memories, and I often wondered if Brad would survive the turbulent skies of the Middle East.

One morning after Dan had returned to the Donjek, I was hurrying to work. The sky was a smoky pink as the sun struggled to rise, and suddenly I thought of Brad again and The Valley. There was a short footbridge over a creek with hand rails on either side, and, as I crossed the bridge a bolt of intuition hit me. My trip to The Valley was certain . . . as certain as my footsteps on the wooden planks of the bridge. It was a revelation that, for a moment, took my breath away. I didn't know when or how I would go, but I *knew* that I would see The Valley. I'd never given up my dream of touching, with my own hands, those ghost ships of another world, and yet, this sudden knowledge that I would actually see them was the first positive feeling I had had about my adventure since Brad had left. I walked to work — into the sunrise. It was symbolic of my dream, rising in the hands of Fate.

* * *

In a month Dan and I moved into a four-room apartment, partially furnished by the Army. It was wonderful to step back into the twentieth century again — oil heat and running water. There was only one shadow of yesterday that disturbed us. The Army had supplied each apartment with a wood-burning kitchen range.

In the six weeks we had lived in Whiskey Flats, we had had enough of wood-chopping. We both recalled how we'd wielded an axe in the dark, after hurrying home from work; how ice had covered the wood and chopping block, and how a north wind had often tried to tear the clothes off our backs while we gathered firewood. With all of this etched into our memories, we went out and purchased an electric kitchen range from the Northern Commercial Company store downtown. We left the wood-burning monster hooked up, however, because I had not forgotten the failure of the oil furnaces in Seventeen. Before the old year rang out, the Army banned the further use of electric stoves in apartments due to fear of an overload on the power plant.

The apartment buildings were like long, one-story barracks with three apartments in each unit. The floors were cold in the winter because the insulation between ground and floor was inadequate. However, each was self-sufficient and private unless neighbors threw rowdy parties, and then the rafters nearly caved in.

* * *

Jim and Georgie had gone to Edmonton for a vacation, and shortly after we were settled in our new place they returned. They came over to visit us one evening carrying a *baby*.

"This is Brooks Keddell," said Georgie, offering the bundle to me.

"We hid things pretty well, didn't we?" Jim murmured, tongue in cheek.

"Gawd . . . you sure did," I said, studying the baby's round little face and bright blue eyes. I slipped him out of his bunting bag and challenged the proud parents. "Look . . . he's beautiful, but . . . he's all of six months. What goes on?"

"He's nine months," corrected Georgie, "and we haven't been

*New father Jim Keddell holds his adopted son, James
Brooks, in 1949.*

married quite a year."

They settled down and told us they had adopted the baby in
Edmonton.

"We really didn't plan to adopt, but, we went to the Children's
Aid, kind of thinking about it, and they let us see Brooks, and
that was it," said Georgie.

"And . . . the CAS couldn't find a baptism certificate for him.
So . . . how would you two like to be godparents?" asked Jim.

James Brooks Keddell was baptized the following Sunday afternoon. The sun shone with a brilliance, lighting up the interior
of the Roman Catholic Mission church in Whitehorse as Dan and
I took turns holding the chubby little fellow. His bright eyes
followed every movement by the priest. Now and again he reached
out with a quick hand to hurry the procedure by lifting up the
holy utensils at the baptismal font. He didn't cry when water was
poured on his head. He just looked startled.

We went back to our apartment to celebrate the baptism with
wine. Georgie and Jim suddenly took on new dimensions. Parent-
hood suited them. Jim spoke with great pride of "his son," and
he and Georgie talked excitedly of plans for his education.

We didn't know then that tragedy lay ahead for Brooks. Before
he was two he would have epileptic seizures, and by the time he
was twenty he would be confined to an institution for life.

Although they had a beautiful daughter of their own a few years
later, they grieved about Brooks. At a later date I heard Georgie
lament, "It would have been better if he'd never been born."

Chapter 31

November was a cold, gray month. Dan came home from the Donjek one day and stayed long enough to pack a few clothes and board a plane for Fort St. John.

At Mile 35, about fifteen miles south of Fort St. John, the Peace River suspension bridge — 2,130 feet long — was having problems. Built in four months in 1942 under supervision of the U.S. Army, the bridge spanned deep, troubled waters. The river had eroded a wide valley in the clay-shale formation in the vicinity of the bridge. The Pine River joined the Peace about a mile upstream. At its confluence with the Peace, the Pine was about 500 feet wide. It was subject to unpredictable flash floods and ice jams that backed up and put a strain on the north anchor block of the bridge.

The Peace River suspension bridge had a main span of 930 feet, suspended side spans of 465 feet, and simple truss spans of 135 feet joining the cable bents to the anchorages.

For several months a Montreal engineering firm, under supervision of the Canadian Army, had been struggling to prevent further movement in the vicinity of the north anchor block. Interlocking sheet piling had been built like a square box around the foundation of the north pier. It was Dan's job to supervise the lowering of buckets of wet cement by crane to a crew below, who dumped the cement into this cofferdam. Also, the Army placed 4,000 tons of 5-ton boulders in the river upstream from the north block, to prevent the backward coiling of the current.

Three years later the Canadian Army tried again to prevent more movement of the north block by depositing in the river 25,000 pieces of concrete, each weighing 300 pounds. But all efforts seemed only to delay by a few years the final demise of the bridge.

On October 15, 1957, close to midnight, a truck driver crossing the bridge noticed an unusual gap in the road near the north anchor block. The bridge was closed to traffic at 8 a.m., October 16, and at noon that day the structure collapsed with a crash of steel and concrete.

The original Peace River suspension bridge was constructed by the U.S. Army Engineers in 1942. The swift Peace River current caused erosion around the north anchor block of the bridge. In 1948 and 1951, the Canadian Army struggled to prevent the resultant shifting of the block, but, in October, 1957, the bridge collapsed.

Photo by James Quong.

While Dan worked at the Peace bridge, I spent all my spare time doing research on an early trailblazer named Jack Dalton who lived in Haines, Alaska (then called Pyramid Harbor) during the gold rush days of 1897 to 1898. Dalton blazed a pioneer trail from Pyramid to Fort Selkirk, near the confluence of the Pelly and Yukon Rivers. The route wove its way for 350 miles through mountains that stood 4,000 feet high.

In the summer of 1898, Dalton supervised the unloading of 300 head of cattle from an ocean freighter at Pyramid. He had purchased the herd in Oregon the previous autumn, and arranged for their freight up the Inside Passage from Seattle. With the help of a dozen friends he drove the cattle over the trail, in the hope of selling beef at $10 a pound on the hoof to starving miners in Dawson. Stories vary on how many emaciated animals reached their destination. A few old-timers said, back in the late 1940s, that 100 survived the trek. Others said a mere 50 survived. The trail was strewn with the rotting bones of animals that had slipped from rocky slopes into gulleys.

Dalton paused at Selkirk with his herd. Selkirk was then an Indian village and trading centre. Traces of an old Hudson's Bay fort built in 1848 and destroyed by Indians in 1852 were still there. A small Roman Catholic mission church, a pioneer cabin that housed a small detachment of Mounties, and a scattering of Indian brush tents made up the rest of the settlement.

Dalton and his cowboys cut trees from the bush and built rafts which he used to float his herd 178 miles downriver to Dawson. The rafts arrived in the Gold City shortly before freeze-up, the swarthy, stalky trailblazer and his friends flogging the skeleton-like animals to take the last steps from raft to land. The town was bursting at the seams with goldseekers who were eager to pay $10 a pound on the hoof for the animals. However, it is said that after paying his cowboys and freight charges Dalton barely broke even on the big venture that was supposed to have made him a million.

He charged a toll for the use of his trail, and he did not hesitate to enforce it with a gun. He was an excellent shot and he didn't like to be argued with.

There was little written on Dalton, and what was recorded was scattered in various newspapers, magazines and books.

* * *

Dan was away often that winter of 1948 to 1949, and I spent every spare moment struggling with my research. I also felt confident enough to write my first novel. For a couple of years, the idea for a novel set in the West and North had been spinning around in my head. At last I put pen to paper and created Natalka Wisnowski, a young immigrant from the Ukraine, who wanted to lose her Ukrainian identity in the new world. Jack Douglas, a U.S. soldier helping to build the Alaska Highway, fell in love with Nat, married her and moved her from Edmonton to Whitehorse. Jealousy, attempted murder and the bittersweet thread of tradition swirled around these two. I loved every minute of that first effort to write a novel that would take me years to hone into shape.

Dan came home on Christmas Day. He missed my frustrated efforts to get a 23-pound turkey ready for a big Yule dinner. The day before Christmas, I had frantically called Al LeClair, who once told me he knew all about cooking turkeys.

"What do I do with this big fowl?" I wailed.

He came over to the apartment, helped me clean the bird and make the dressing, and gave me instructions on how to cook it.

"You start the old wood-burner," he said. "Early tomorrow."

"What?" I cried with concern. "We can't even regulate that old oven."

"It cooks better than all those new fandangle things. My mother, back in Quebec, always used an old wood-burner. The flavor of everything is preserved, like . . . Oo-la-la."

He rolled his big brown eyes. Al was a bit of a clown. He and his girl friend, Ella Halfyard, and I often went fishing together in the summer months; Al knew how to cook a fresh fish so it made your taste buds sing.

I fired up the old wood-burner early Christmas morning, and thought that at least the people running the power plant would be proud of me. And, Al was right. Christmas dinner, plum pudding and all, turned out like a gourmet feast. Twelve of us, including Al, Ella, Tudy and others, sang Christmas carols, drank Christmas wine and ate up a storm.

* * *

In the new year, I was offered a job with the U.S. Army Corps of Engineers which took care of the pipeline from Skagway (at the head of the Inside Passage) to Anchorage and Fairbanks, 600 miles northwest of Whitehorse. I had been with Reemee 2½ years and I felt like moving on to something else. Also, the

U.S. job offered me $65 a month more than I had been getting with the Canadian Army.

A hazy twilight hugged the refinery grounds at 5 p.m. on the day I said "goodbye" to Blatchford.

"Of course, you'll be around Whitehorse, and certainly, I'll be around. We'll see one another in passing, if nothing else . . . or, please feel free to visit my wife and me. Anytime," he said.

That was the last time I saw him. A couple of months later he left Whitehorse and took his discharge from the Army. There were reports that he was working as equipment engineer with the Bechtel Mannix firm, contractors for the Interprovincial Pipeline in Alberta. A little over a year later I read the notice of his death, at forty-two, in the *Edmonton Journal*. I thought it was strange that he died on the same day (the 22nd) of the same month (April) that his father had disappeared. The two deaths were seventeen years apart — Jim Blatchford in 1950, and his father in 1933.

I asked friends and acquaintances what had happened to Blatch to cause his death. Nobody knew. Thirty-two years later I wrote to the Alberta Department of Vital Statistics to request his death certificate. A department official said he would send me the certificate if I would send a fee of $3. I sent the fee, and within two weeks it was returned to me with a typed note that said: "Please be advised that this division cannot issue a death certificate for the above noted James Walker Blatchford."

Years ago the cause of Jim Blatchford's death was a mystery to me, and today it remains a mystery.

General Walsh put Blatchford's drinking problem into perspective for me in December, 1982, as follows: "As to his drinking, I found that as long as he was kept busy and had a challenge, he seemed to be able to control it. I recall on one occasion I wanted to see him about something and it took two days to get hold of him, and when I did, I took him off on a fishing trip, would not let him have anything to drink until night when I allowed him a couple (of drinks) before our evening meal. He was perfectly normal in a couple of days and we did not have any trouble with him for some time. He was a very capable officer."

* * *

Early in January of 1949 Dan began to put together supplies for a 150-mile expedition on snowshoes across the Haines Road. When the U.S. Army Engineers built the Alaska Highway, they put this spur route into the small fishing village of Haines. The Haines Road followed, in part, the old Dalton Trail. Until the road went through, the village had only one route — by sea — to the outside world. Although a great boon to progress in the summer months, the road was useless in the wintertime when snow drifted in through the mountain passes and closed the route, isolating the village.

Dan, along with L/Cpl. Donald Croft, was commissioned to record the wind velocity, temperature and depth of snow at strategic places along the road, with a view to keeping the route open year-round.

We arose at five o'clock on a bitter-cold morning in mid-February. Our outside thermometer said 18 below zero and a wind screeched around the corners of the building. Dan packed personal items — extra socks, underwear, ski pants, parka — in a pack sack, then we had breakfast and waited for the arrival of the Army truck, which would be carrying sled dogs, an RCMP freight toboggan, rations for a week for men and dogs, sleeping bags, silk tent, first-aid chest, and extra snowshoes. When the truck arrived just before six o'clock, Paddy Jim, a 21-year-old Indian guide (whose wife had presented him with a baby boy the day before) jumped out of the cab along with the driver.

"We make good time. You see," said Paddy.

I was doubtful about "good time" as I stood, huddled in parka and heavy ski pants, trying not to breathe too deeply of the bitter-cold air that stung my lungs.

As Dan and Croft checked supplies for the last time, to make sure they had everything they had ordered, Jim Keddell came zooming up in a jeep.

"We'll fly over in an Air Force plane, every day. You signal in the snow. Right?"

"Right."

"You know the signals for OK and trouble?"

"Yeah . . . yeah. We're not stupid, Keddell." Dan sounded impatient.

"I suppose you're pretty good on snowshoes now. Both of you." Keddell looked from Croft to Dan and back again.

"Pretty damn good. Went ten miles yesterday, tramping through the bush. I think I can outrun you."

"That's for damshur." Keddell laughed.

Suddenly they were gone. I stood, shivering in the wind that threatened to lift me into the air like a kite. I watched the truck rumble along, turn a corner and disappear.

"Nothing to worry about," said Jim. "Look . . . I'll be in touch with you every day, tell you of their progress."

Jim kept his word. Each day he came over to the apartment,

167

told me he'd been up in the RCAF Norseman, had seen the signal in the snow telling the outside world the little party was okay. When Dan returned, however, he said he had not seen the plane, and Jim, tongue in cheek, said he and the pilot had searched in vain for the little party.

"Never once saw even a trace of you. Where the hell did ya get to?"

"Somewhere . . . in that big, mean world out there," said Dan. "By God, a life could be snuffed out so quickly you'd never even find a ghost."

Georgie interviewed Dan, and, in a subsequent story in the *Whitehorse Star,* said the following:

> "The path that Cameron and his party took traverses country of unsurpassed scenery and breath-taking ruggedness. Men have died on that trail, seeking an easier route into the Klondike gold fields. The same howling wind that nagged at nerves of the restless gold seekers, was blowing when the engineers' little party passed through the Haines Road last week.
>
> "Southwest 35 miles per hour," is noted in Cameron's log book. "But we bent our heads and headed into her. We made camp early that first night. It looked like a blizzard and we were taking no chances."

Through the narrow passes, the snow measured eighteen feet deep. As the men neared the coast, the weather became warmer and more humid, and the snow became heavy and built up on their snowshoes.

"Each time we lifted a foot, it was like lifting a ten-ton weight," said Dan, whose ankles swelled to twice their size from the strain.

In Haines, Dan chartered a fishing boat that took them 15 miles across the canal to Skagway, where they mounted everything — dogs, toboggan and gear — on the train and returned to Whitehorse.

The following winter, Army road equipment moved in and kept the Haines Road open, and it has been kept open in winter and summer ever since.

Pausing briefly, Dan Cameron stands next to his dog team during a week-long trek over the Haines Road in the winter of 1948 to 1949. With an Indian guide and provisions to last eight days, Cameron studied weather conditions along the snow-covered road. His researches assisted the Canadian Army in making plans to keep the route open in the winter months.

Chapter 32

The winter of 1948 to 1949 was a depressing one for Georgina and me. We had gradually learned that although we were civilians, we were governed by the same Army rules and regulations that applied to our husbands.

I found myself sitting beside an attractive blond woman on the Army bus one Saturday afternoon. I hadn't seen her before, and I asked her if she were a new arrival in Whitehorse. She told me she had been there for two weeks, had come from Ottawa, and her husband was a captain with the Engineers.

"My husband doesn't want me to speak to the wives of men who are subordinate to him," she said, before our conversation had gone far.

"Well . . . I'm not subordinate to him," I said.

"But your husband is."

"Only in rank," I persisted, realizing that she must know Dan and me better than I knew her.

As I sat in silence beside this rather haughty individual, I decided she would make a good character in a story, and later she became a provocative antagonist in a short story that I titled "Blond Goddesses are Rare." The story sold to a slick farm monthly in Ohio.

The bus incident was minor, but it pointed up a major wall that boxed people in. Looking back from an era that launched the Feminist Movement, I note that we women of earlier times were seen by society as "possessions" of our husbands. The Army was no exception, and to make matters worse, the Army was set up like a medieval feudal system. It promoted a lord-to-vassal arrangement in human relations. At that time, too, there was a shift in the old guard (the pioneers who had come in 1946 to launch the Northwest Highway System). Walsh had been gone for more than a year, Major Lovatt-Fraser had left on posting, Blatchford and MacKay had chosen civvy street, Flora MacDonald had left to take a job with the Alberta government, Rena was working for Ma Murray in Fort St. John. The new people coming

The young soldiers Sgt. Dan Cameron, left, and Lt. Bill Moore were in charge of the Canadian Army's first major road-building project — from the Alaska Highway into the town of Atlin, British Columbia. They are studying the specs and countryside for the last fifteen miles of the road.

in seemed to smack of boot polish and protocol. Georgie and I felt dissatisfied with Army life. A strange boredom began to settle into our bones.

I talked to Dan one evening about my feelings, and he said that he, too, had known this same uneasiness. In fact, he'd been thinking of taking his discharge from the Army.

"The oil fields are booming in Alberta. I think there should be a great career out there," he said.

However, we were well aware that the moment to make a move had not yet arrived. For one thing, The Valley was still out there somewhere, awaiting my "touch." I could never leave until my quest was over, the Holy Grail in my slim hands.

I continued to work for the U.S. Army Engineers where I had made friends with the half-dozen office workers and thirty members of the maintenance crew that took care of the long pipeline. My job was typing and shorthand, and compiling reports on the number of gallons of oil used per month, the number of gallons in dozens of storage tanks scattered along the route, and the number of gallons in the line.

* * *

In March, Dan was informed that he would be second in command of a major road-building project — a sixty-mile gravel road that would link the town of Atlin, in northern British Columbia, with the Alaska Highway. Lieut. Bill Moore, R.C.E., was in charge of the project. Contracts had been arranged with several Yukon construction firms to put machinery and operators to work on the road in June. This machinery would be supplemented by heavy equipment from the Army.

On June 7, a camp for 130 workers was completed at Jakes Corner, fify miles south of Whitehorse, where the road to Carcross joined the Alaska Highway. The new road would make a branch off the Carcross Road close to Jakes Corner.

The Atlin Road was the first major road-building project undertaken by the Northwest Highway System, and Dan was proud that he had been chosen to be a part of it. Also, he would be closer to Whitehorse than he had been at the Donjek, and his work as "expeditor" would be a challenge. As plans for the road unfolded, he realized he would be responsible for coordinating the flow of materials to the job site. This almost cost him his life at one stage along the way, but he didn't know about the near-tragedy that lay ahead when, in June, the first Cats moved in on the dense forest near Jakes Corner.

The town of Atlin, 110 miles southwest of Whitehorse, was then a community of 300 hardy residents, huddled on the shore of Atlin Lake. The town and its surrounding country were accessible only by pack train, bush plane or boat across lakes and inlets to the White Pass and Yukon Route Railroad at Carcross, about seventy miles away.

Secretary of the Atlin Historical Society, Diane S. Smith, in a letter to me in July, 1982, said: "The building of the Atlin Road brought an end to the total isolation that people had lived with from the founding of the community in 1898. I can certainly understand why they felt like kicking up their heels when they finally had a tie with the outside world, any time of the year, at only the cost of a tank of gasoline."

The name Atlin comes from the Indian word "aht-lah," meaning "big water." Atlin Lake is sixty miles long and from two to five miles wide. Surveyors put the site of the new road along the edge of this lake. From the southwestern tip of Atlin Lake almost to the seacoast at Juneau sprawls the magnificent Llewellyn Glacier. The Atlin country has been called "Switzerland of the North" by mountain climbers, geologists and gold seekers.

In the spring and summer of 1898, hundreds of men worked on the building of the White Pass and Yukon Route Railroad that would, by 1900, link Skagway with Whitehorse. In July and August of 1898 there were wild cries of "gold in Atlin." Railroad workers not only left their jobs to trek overland to the new gold fields, but they took their picks and shovels with them.

* * *

Atlin is also linked with aviation history; the first air-rescue efforts in British Columbia and the Yukon were worldwide news following the disappearance of veteran Atlin bush pilot E.J.A. (Paddy) Burke in 1930.

Burke, an Irishman who had flown for twelve years with the Royal Flying Corps, and who had chalked up 2,500 hours in thirty-seven different types of planes, applied for the Air-Land job at Atlin in 1928. He was hired and moved from England to the remote B.C. town with his wife and two small children.

On October 11, 1930, Burke was hired to take trapper Robert Marten on a flight from Atlin to Lower Liard Post, about 200 miles east. Emil Kading, a mechanic, accompanied the two. Since it was a routine flight, not too far away, and the weather still sang of Indian summer, the trio carried few provisions. Their sleeping bags were summer issue, and they had the following supplies: 50 pounds of dried beans, 3 tins of bully beef, 1 pound of tea, 3 pounds of sugar and raisins, 3 tins of dried vegetables and 2 pounds of butter. They carried a single rifle and twelve rounds of ammunition. The plane was still mounted on pontoons.

They landed at Lower Liard Post, spent the night there and started back for Atlin the following day. An hour away from the post, Burke ran into a blizzard. There were no radios or radio ranges in that territory in those days, and Burke, flying by the seat of his pants, knew that he had to get out of the zero visibility. The only way to go was to land, and he could barely see the Liard River as he brought the plane in and taxied along the water. It was a good landing, but he did not see a submerged log. It punctured both pontoons and the plane slowly sank in three feet of water. Even if the men had carried strong ropes and pulleys, they still could not have raised the craft to fix the pontoons because the river banks were too steep to permit that kind of salvage work. The cabin of the plane was not underwater, so they threw a wooden plank to the land and deserted the ship. In the nearby trees they built a fire and camped, hoping for rescue. By October 17, their small cache of food ran out. The river had iced over, and the pontoons, bedded down in the ice, looked hopelessly locked in. The men decided to leave the area. They headed, on foot, for Junkers Lake, sixty miles upriver, where they knew a cache of food lay.

When Paddy had not returned by October 15, his wife alerted headquarters of the Air-Land Company he worked for in Vancouver. A search aircraft was dispatched that day from Vancouver, but it crashed on take-off, with damage to the plane but no injuries to the pilot and his mechanic. Another plane went up immediately, but, since nobody knew where Burke had gone down, the search was conducted 100 miles off-base for a week, then was abandoned.

In the meantime, the men walked along the river bank, which was rugged and difficult terrain for their light, summer shoes. The ice of the river was too weak in places to permit them to take the river route. Game was not plentiful, and, after their food ran out, they bagged one duck and three small squirrels, which turned out to be their only sustenance in a three-week period. About November 18, Kading managed to kill a caribou with the second-to-last shot in his rifle, but the kill came too late. Although he made soup in an old gasoline can (the only cooking pot they had), Paddy Burke was too far gone to digest the food and he died two days later.

By October 26, when the men had not been located, Pat Renahan, an old friend of Burke's in Seattle, became concerned. He obtained permission from his employer, Alaska Washington Airways, to go on the search. Frank Hatcher, Renahan's mechanic, was only twenty-one, but he had logged hundreds of hours in the air in Alaska.

Probably the search would never have hit headlines around the world if Renahan and Hatcher had made the trip alone. At the last minute, Sam Clerf went along as a guide, and Sam, a mine owner and rancher, was well-known in Washington, Alaska and British Columbia. The story of Burke had not even been mentioned in most Canadian and American newspapers, although a few small-town papers had carried a one-paragraph account of the downed plane on inside pages.

Renahan, Hatcher and Clerf left Seattle early on October 28 and stayed overnight at Butedale, B.C., a coastal town near Prince

Knocking down timber, a bulldozer clears a right-of-way for the road from the Alaska Highway to Atlin.

Rupert. Here they refuelled and took off for Ketchikan, Alaska. They were never seen or heard of again.

When Renahan's plane didn't appear in Ketchikan, newspapers picked up the story of the missing mine owner and rancher. The governments of Canada and the United States took notice, especially when the double plane loss was written up as the worst tragedy in Alaska-Yukon aviation history, only a year after Carl Ben Eielson, king of flying in Alaska, went down in Siberia.

Dozens of privately owned planes began a search for Burke and Renahan. The Canadian government put two Fairchilds into the air, and the U.S. Navy sent two Loening amphibians from San Diego. They combed coastal areas and inland areas for two weeks in a diligent, systematic search, but all to no avail. Finally, everybody gave up, including the two governments — everybody except Everett L. Wasson, a husky 24-year-old pilot with Treadwell-Yukon Company, along with Alex Crone as mechanic and prospector Joe Walsh as guide.

Wasson left Whitehorse on November 12, after his Fairchild was fitted with skis. He decided on a systematic sweep of the hazardous terrain between Atlin and Liard Post — an unmapped wilderness with 8,000-foot-high mountain peaks. The

New road to Atlin winds along ahead of a Canadian Army truck in November, 1949. Atlin Lake glimmers in the distance.

temperature had dipped to thirty below zero and fierce storms swooped down from the top of the world.

Wasson made so many landings in the bush area that he lost count. He and his passengers had to stamp out emergency runways with snowshoes for take-offs, and Walsh ran beside the plane to lighten the load, then hopped on and climbed in as the aircraft began to lift.

On December 4 they spotted Burke's Junkers, and two days later, still doggedly following the trail, they found the downed men. Kading and Marten were whiskered skeletons, too weak to stand. Wasson cooked rations he had brought from Whitehorse, and around a roaring campfire they ate and were packed into winter sleeping bags until, two days later, they were able to stagger to the Fairchild, ten miles away.

On December 19, Wasson, Walsh and a Royal Canadian Mounted Police sergeant named Leopold flew back for Burke's body. The pilot arrived home for a sad, Christmas burial, and the people of Atlin have erected a propeller off a Junkers aircraft to mark his grave.

The Renahan search yielded nothing. Fifteen months later, two wheels off the aircraft were found near Point Davidson on Annette Island. Shortly before this a piece of wood with blue fabric attached to it was found and identified as part of Renahan's Vega aircraft.

* * *

That spring, summer and autumn of 1949, a gravel road slowly took form across the mountains where Paddy Burke had flown his Junkers and Everett Wasson had conducted his heroic search-rescue. The road would eventually link this colorful, historic country with the outside world.

While Dan was busy making history, I continued my work by day at the bright, modern offices of the U.S. Army Corps of Engineers in Upper Whitehorse. At night I delved into my research on the Yukon's wild trailblazer — Jack Dalton.

Dan came home an odd weekend with stories of The Road, and one weekend told me a chilling story of an adventure that nearly ended in disaster.

Chapter 33

"You wouldn't believe what happened last week. Jeez . . ." Dan's voice was strained.

It was a Friday night in July, about ten o'clock. I was reading at the kitchen table when he opened the door, stepped in, put his packsack on the floor, sagged into a chair, and lit a cigarette.

"What happened?" I asked.

"Well . . . Bill and I realized last Thursday that we were running low on dynamite supplies, and we knew of a cache that had belonged to the Americans, only it was three hundred miles down the road."

"Near Lower Post?"

Dan nodded. "I offered to go and get the stuff, and Cody, an engineering student from Alberta, asked if he could come with me. I didn't mind the company, so we drove down to the site, an Army demolition dump, and we loaded a ton and a half of dynamite on the back of a truck."

"A ton and a half?" I gulped, thinking it was a lot of dynamite.

"A ton and a half," Dan echoed. "That's not much when you're bulldozing a road through mountains. Well, anyway, just before we left, I threw a box of caps into the glove compartment."

He paused.

"Caps and dynamite together? Is that good?" I asked.

"It's against regulations and I knew it. The dynamite is fairly stable, but the caps are a highly sensitive explosive, easily set off by shock or heat. But, you see, I was taking chances because I didn't want to go back again the next day to get the caps. Cody drove, and all was OK until we came to one of those long, steep, winding switchbacks. Jaysus! He lost his brakes, was doing seventy. We were plunging like a rocket down that hill when he pulled the emergency brake. We slowed to fifty . . . Gawd . . . fifty? Still too fast for gearing down."

"Scary."

"Scary as hell. We rocked around curves. Cody tried t' keep the outfit upright. Then the emergency brake caught fire. Flames

178

licked and snapped under the floorboards at my feet. I could see smoke streaming out the back. I thought of those goddam caps. I was wishing I hadn't put them in, but I didn't have to worry too long. Cody never made the next switchback. Suddenly we were in the ditch, plunging from one side to the other —"

"Why didn't you jump?"

"I thought of it, believe me . . . but we were going too fast, all over the place, until the truck straddled the edge of the road. The front axle dragged along the berm and the resistance pulled us to a stop."

"Then you ran?"

"No. We scooped up gravel with our hands from the side of the road, threw it on the burning brake until the fire went out, then we ran about five hundred yards to the top of a hill where we sat and smoked cigarettes."

"Wow."

"When we realized the outfit wasn't going to blow, we went back, got water from a creek nearby to get the brakes working, then we *drove* back onto the road."

"And . . . *no* damage at all?"

"The floorboards were charred right through in a couple of places. That was it."

"And you kept the caps?"

He looked at me wide-eyed. "You can't just throw caps out anywhere, or even bury them. There are laws on that. They have to be detonated."

"That's right. I forgot," I sighed, relieved I hadn't known about this escapade when it was happening. He sat before me, all in one piece, and I thanked God the whole outfit hadn't gone skyward. I shuddered to think there wouldn't have been a tiny piece left of either Dan or Cody if this had happened.

Cody, a third-year student in engineering, switched to teaching when he went back to university. He sent Dan a Christmas card every year for years afterwards, with a short note, "Remember me?"

* * *

In June of that year, about a month before this near-disaster, a federal election put Louis St. Laurent, Canada's second French-Canadian prime minister, back into power. Mackenzie King had resigned in November, 1948, in favor of St. Laurent. On June 27, I was amazed at the line-up of Indians at the polling booth on Main Street. Treaty Indians did not receive full franchise to vote in a federal election until July 1, 1960. The Yukon Indians, however, were *not* treaty Indians, and they could and did vote in every federal election, as long as they could travel to the nearest polling booth.

The Liberals won a victory that year unparalled in Canadian history — 193 seats in the House — making it the only party with a solid base in every region of Canada.

The Territorial Government of the Yukon held an election every three years, and 1949 was not an election year. The governing body was composed of a controller who was appointed by the federal government, and an elected legislative council of three members. The Yukon Territorial Council and the Controller operated in a manner similar to a provincial government.

In 1949 the territory was divided into three electoral districts — Dawson, Mayo and Whitehorse. The Territorial Council members elected in 1947 were John R. Fraser for Dawson; Ernest J. Corp for Mayo; and R. Gordon Lee, Whitehorse.

* * *

During the summer of 1949, the Keddells left Whitehorse for Fort St. John, where Georgie went to work on the newspaper with her mother. Jim took his discharge from the Army, and worked for several companies in construction and exploration for oil.

I felt lonely when they left and took a vacation, going to Edmonton where Dad and I drove out to his cottage at Lac Ste. Anne. In Whitehorse, Tudy, Win, Rena and I had often gone swimming in Eyre Lake, which was located about three miles from Whitehorse. Eyre was one of the few spring-fed lakes and it was not as cold or life-threatening as the ones fed from melting ice in the mountains. However, Lac Ste. Anne seemed like a bathtub to me, by comparison, and in a week I acquired a tan, went fishing often with my father, and talked at great length with him and his mother, Melvina Morritt. My grandmother and my dad urged me to write of my many experiences in the Yukon. They were people who believed that Canadian history was exciting, dramatic, full of intrigue and colorful personalities.

"Write it the way it is," they urged. "Write it."

* * *

When I came back to Whitehorse in September, Dan informed me he had asked for a transfer to Camp Borden, Ontario, where he hoped to get his discharge.

"We'll be leaving as soon as the Atlin Road is finished, probably late November," he said.

I had always planned to visit Martha Louise Black, who had climbed the Chilkoot Pass and followed gold seekers into Dawson City in 1898. She had written an enthralling autobiography, *My Seventy Years*, and a book titled *Yukon Wild Flowers*.

Martha's husband, George Black, had been a lawyer in Dawson around the turn of the century. He was elected to the Territorial Council in 1905 and appointed Commissioner of the Yukon in 1912. This office of Commissioner was abolished in 1918 by an Order in Council, and the duties were transferred to the Gold Commissioner and later the Controller.

In those early days, Martha Black had been a gracious hostess at Government House in Dawson. Her husband had been a Federal member of Parliament for the Yukon from 1921 to 1935. In 1935, when he was speaker of the House of Commons, he became ill and resigned his position. Mrs. Black, however, ran in his place and was elected.

In her autobiography, she said: "I made my maiden speech in the House of Commons at the age of seventy."

On a bright Saturday afternoon in September, I knocked at a side door of the Black home, which faced the river. George — tall, friendly — answered.

"I've always wanted to meet your wife, and since I'll be leaving Whitehorse soon, I wondered . . ."

He interrupted. "Come in . . . come in."

He reached out and drew me inside with a gentle arm. "Please sit down." He indicated a Chesterfield in a large living room, which was tastefully furnished in modern style. "She'll be with you in a minute."

Rows of books in bookcases caught my eye, and a bright bouquet of wild flowers graced an oak table in an adjoining dining room. Mrs. Black came in a few minutes later, smiling warmly, a hand extended for a gracious, friendly handshake.

She was in her eighties then — a short, frail-looking woman with bright blue eyes.

"I'm Hope Morritt. I'm interested in writing, have had a little published, have read your books and loved them."

She smiled, sat down and motioned for me to sit again. "You're living in Whitehorse?"

"Yes. I'm working for the U.S. Army Engineers, and I've been here three years."

"Three years!" She leaned forward in her chair. "But, why didn't you come around to see me sooner?"

181

Carrying a basket brimming with flowers, Martha Black stands with her husband, George Black, in a garden. The year was 1935.

Photo courtesy MacBride Museum Collection/Yukon Archives.

"I didn't know you personally, and I hesitated. Then, when I learned last week that my husband, who's in the Army, will be transferred to Ontario soon, I decided to knock at your door, take a chance on meeting you."

"I'm glad you came. What a pity you're leaving. Have you enjoyed working in the Yukon?"

"Loved it, but . . . I often think that I was born too late. For instance, I'd have loved your era . . . gold and all the excitement that gold creates."

"But every age has its excitement. What could be more of a challenge than bulldozing a road through eighteen hundred miles of wilderness? And . . . all in the short span of nine months? A birth . . . an exciting birth of a new era in the Far North. You know, when we scrambled over the Pass years ago, we never thought there'd be a railroad over that trail a few years later. And a road that would link us with the outside world wasn't even a wild dream."

We talked excitedly for two hours — about books, the Klondike, colorful characters she knew, politics — then a slim young Indian woman brought tea.

"I like you," she said as I was about to take my leave. *"Please,*, if you ever come back to Whitehorse, come and see me. No invitation is needed, other than that."

A few days later I received a small booklet in the mail, titled *A Klondike Christmas Tale*, by Martha Louise Black, O.B.E., F.R.G.S. Across the title page, in bold, black pen, she had made the note "This was my Christmas greeting to friends last year."

* * *

In October and November I saw little of Dan, as the engineers were hurrying to finish the road before winter set in.

On a crisp, sunny afternoon in October, I looked up from my desk at the office to see Bob Smith.

"You're back again, photographing the country?" I asked.

He nodded. Bob reminded me of Tim. His Air Force cap was always bashed out of shape from wearing earphones. There was a quiet confidence in the slow, easy smile. He wasn't as cocky as Tim had been, however, and he wasn't the daredevil that Tim had been. I still remembered Bob's comment on the flight to Watson Lake, "There are old pilots and bold pilots, but there are no old, bold pilots."

"Do you remember telling me about Million Dollar Valley?" he asked.

"I sure do. Have you found it?"

He nodded. "We're going out there tomorrow. Would you like to come?"

It seemed so sudden that for a moment I couldn't find words to reply. The climax to a dream. The Valley . . . again within reach.

"Would I like to come? Yes . . . yes . . . yes."

"Good. You know, Hope, I couldn't forget that valley, ever since you told me about those bombers. I've been looking for it, asking about it. Last week we flew over, and it's something. How those Marauders ever got in there, intact, I'll never know."

He paused, shook his head incredulously.

"Will you land?" I asked breathlessly, "near the bombers?"

His eyes widened with alarm. "Never. That's impossible country."

"And then, there's a strange gravitational pull."

I paused as he studied me astutely. "Pull?"

"You didn't feel it when you flew over?"

"Do you believe in that science fiction stuff we hear about the Bermuda Triangle?"

"No."

"OK." He shrugged as though to denote that the same principle applied in The Valley. I wasn't convinced.

"Look, if the weather's good, bright, clear like now, we'll leave at ten in the morning. If it's foggy, really foggy . . . like visibility zero, we're grounded."

"I'll meet you at the airport. Ten o'clock tomorrow morning. It'll be clear. It's got to be."

"OK. See you."

I slept fitfully that night, lost in a cloud of dreams and nightmares. I saw a room lit with coal oil lamps, period furniture, a man sitting at an old piano . . . a torch singer leaning against the piano belting out soul music. Every time I reached out to touch the singer, she vanished. The man, too, vanished, and the piano exploded just before my fingertips touched the cold white keys.

The next day was cloudless, clear, with an Indian summer sun warming everything it touched. I took the day off from work, called a cab and arrived at the airport as the crew was getting into the Dak. At ten-thirty we roared down the runway for take-off. We flew east and south. I sat in the cockpit with the crew. I'd never seen the country so beautiful, a bright sun spotlighting the jagged mountain peaks and patches of sunlight playing in mottled grandeur across the valleys. Nature was making every effort to make the day perfect.

After an hour and a half, Bob told me we were coming close to The Valley. The co-pilot vacated his seat so I could sit there and see better. My heart beat wildly. I'd dreamed of this moment for so long that even as I sat in the co-pilot's seat it seemed unreal. I thought of Brad, who'd made a fortune from the metal off the hulks of those big, sagging birds. I thought of Tim, who'd bought jewelry from Brad . . . Tim, who'd been the first to tell me about The Valley.

"The Valley is my story," he'd said. I realized as I sat in the co-pilot's seat that now it was *my* story . . . all mine, but I could never forget, or leave out of the story, the man who'd first introduced me to the eerie Valley.

We went through turbulence, the Dak shaking and creaking and a white mist rising around it. My hands began to sweat as I remembered again the gravitational pull that Tim once said "Sucked all flying objects into The Valley."

As the plane bounced around in the cloud formations I clung to my chair, seat belt hugging me tightly to the aircraft.

The ground below, appearing through the fog, looked desolate and rugged. Then we were into another patch of fog and I couldn't see the ground. Bob took the ship down to a lower level, but the clouds were dense, packed in like mounds of sheep. He went up to a higher level and cleared the clouds, but now the ghostlike veils were beneath us. He made a dozen passes back and forth. He cussed quietly, reached for dials, trimmed. The big bombers were there, under us, like big sprawling eagles . . . wounded, never to rise again. They were there, but I couldn't see them. Only the sharp mountain peaks were visible through mists, standing like sentries, guarding their treasure.

We crisscrossed The Valley again and again. Mother Earth did not reach out and pull us to her bosom, and the fog did not move.

"Damn . . . damn," said Bob, clucking his tongue in disappointment. "It's too bad you weren't with us last week."

"It *is* too bad," I moaned, feeling disappointment settle like a rock in the pit of my stomach.

When I arrived home in the early afternoon, the sun was still shining in a cloudless sky. Had the gods elected to roll in that fog at that crucial moment so that *I* could not see The Valley? Like Lancelot du Lac, I had the Holy Grail at my fingertips, only for it to slip out of reach, leaving the real world pressing morbidly in.

Chapter 34

Late in November, when only a few miles of the Atlin Road remained to be finished, a deluge of rain and soft snow hit the area. Supply trucks could not run the road without landing in ditches, and all equipment and men were stranded. Bill and Dan were discouraged. It seemed that the final grading of the last few miles into Atlin would have to wait until spring. Then the RCAF came to the rescue by sending a Norseman with supplies into the small landing field in the town. Idle road gangs went back to work and finished the final grading.

On a Saturday night in early December, residents gave a dinner-dance at the Moose Hall in Atlin. The building was packed. A small band kicked out lively dance tunes and overproof rum flowed like maple syrup at a pancake feast.

Early in January, 1950, Dan received a copy of a letter to Brigadier Connelly from the Whitehorse Board of Trade. It read as follows: "At a recent meeting of the Whitehorse Board of Trade, I was asked to write you with regard to the Atlin Road Project. The Board and the general public of Atlin and Whitehorse feel that the Canadian Army and the various departments connected with it, have accomplished an extremely fine job in completing the Atlin Road last year, in the time allotted and with the money afforded them. We therefore extend our heartiest congratulations for the remarkable work performed." The letter was signed by R.J. Rowan, secretary.

On a snowy day in December, Dan and I stood at the railroad station platform surrounded by friends — Tudy, Betty, Win and several of the men who had worked with Dan on the road. It was a tearful farewell, and I remembered Bert Cluett's words, "Don't stay in the Yukon longer'n two years. If ye do an' leave, ye'll always be scratchin' t' come back."

We took the train to Skagway and the boat down the Inside Passage to Vancouver. Through the years, Bert's words have proven to be prophetic. Sometimes I ached with a haunting loneliness to live again in that great rugged land north of the

A smiling group of Whitehorse people poses in front of a sign at Haines Junction on the Alaska Highway. From left: Hazel Stewart, Flora MacDonald, Dora Simpson, Margaret Moses, Fred Haines and Win Haines.

sixtieth. Often, my disappointment at not seeing The Valley rose and lodged, a big lump in my throat. But . . . I thought of Fate and consoled myself that it was meant to be . . . written in the stars.

Afterword

The Northwest Highway System put its indelible stamp on the Alaska Highway. It was the force that kept the road alive and well for eighteen years. A written account of all the bridge-building/road-building projects and the people who made them possible would take volumes, and my original idea in writing this book was not to write a heavy, statistical history. I wanted to write of my memories of the erratic, nervous four-year period following the Second World War, when the Canadian Army first took over the maintenance of 1,221 miles of a military road that wove its precarious way through rugged, mountain terrain. In those years, under the able leadership of Brig. Geoffrey Walsh and Brig. Allan B. Connelly, the Alaska Highway not only thrived, but expanded . . . in spite of obsolete road equipment inherited from the Americans . . . in spite of a meagre federal budget that stipulated "just maintain the road — nothing more."

I tried to include in this book stories of the Far North as they touched my life or sparked my interest. Although it had little link with the NWHS, I had to tell of my search for The Valley that guards the big bombers that lost their way en route from Boise, Idaho, to Ladd Field, near Fairbanks, Alaska.

The Alaska Highway has grown from a fledgling to an adult in the years from 1946 to the launching of this book in 1986. The road is now a permanent artery in Canada. The U.S. Government has been given much praise for the miracle it performed in building the road, and this is only right . . . but we, as Canadians, should not forget the other miracles performed by the Canadian Army in keeping this artery open for nearly a quarter of a century.

There are several plaques commemorating the various stages of growth of the highway, and honoring those people who made this growth possible. The plaques are located on the road near Whitehorse. Three of them read as follows:

On Nov. 20, 1942, the Alaska Highway was completed as a wartime expedient. Today, 25 years later, during the centenaries of Canada and the state of Alaska, this plaque commemorates that event and honors the brave men whose unstinting efforts made the highway a reality and indeed an avenue to the glorious future of Alaska and the Yukon territory.

This monument commemorates 18 years of service on the Alaska Highway by units of the Corps of Royal Canadian Engineers 1946-1964.

At this site on 1 April 1964, the Canadian Army handed over responsibility for the Alaska Highway and the Northwest Highway System to the Federal Department of Public Works.

Today, the road is paved in a most places — less than one hundred miles are gravel. The section in Alaska has been paved for many years, but, since Canada inherited the longest part of the road, paving presented problems. In 1977, the cost of paving one mile was half a million dollars. In the northern section, where permafrost weeps copiously if you touch it with the tip of a shovel, engineers faced further problems. And then, there were people along the road who wanted to keep it gravelled to reflect a still-rugged country. To this hardy group, a windshield peppered with stones was like a trophy telling the world they have travelled the length of the highway and survived.

However, even these hardy sourdoughs had to give in to progress. The northern section of the road is now a ten-year paving project. In a letter to me dated May 8, 1979, Jim Quong, manager Bridges and Special Projects, Public Works Canada, outlined this project as follows: "By agreement between the U.S. and Canadian government, the U.S. will finance the upgrading and paving of the Canada Section of the Haines Road to Haines Junction, and from there to the Alaska-Yukon border at Mile 1221.6 — called the Shakwak Project. The work commenced in 1978 and is expected to be completed within ten years. The project is managed by Public Works Canada, being responsible for all the engineering and construction of about 300 miles of highway including bridge crossings."

* * *

Dan Cameron took his discharge from the Army in 1950 and worked for ten years as supervisor, mechanical equipment, in oil fields in Alberta. In 1960 his company transferred him to Sarnia, Ontario, and in 1981 he became supervisor of one of the oil-drilling camps in the Sahara Desert, with a home base in Ontario.

Ma Murray departed this life at age 95 on September 22, 1982, outliving her son-in-law, Jim Keddell, by two years. Ma died in Lillooet, B.C., surrounded by her loving daughter Georgina, granddaughter Margaret, and great-grandchildren. Just before the end, Ma told her granddaughter that she wanted to be left alone in her room to say her penance. Then she said, "Margie, I hope they open the gates for me."

When I interviewed Geof Walsh in Ottawa in June, 1982, he said, "Our ranks are getting thin. Sarantos and Lovatt-Fraser died in the last two years."

After launching the Northwest Highway System, Walsh moved on to other great accomplishments. He was director-general of military training in Canada from 1953 to 1955; quartermaster-general, 1955 to 1959; general officer commanding Western Command, 1959 to 1961; Chief of the General Staff, October 1961 to August 1964, when he was appointed Vice-Chief Canadian Defence Staff on integration of the three services. He retired from active service in October, 1966, with the rank of lieutenant-general. During the Second World War he won the Distinguished Service Order and was made a Commander of the Order of the British Empire (CBE), Commander U.S. Legion of Merit, and Commander of the Organge Order of Nassau (Netherlands). He was also twice mentioned in dispatches.

Brigadier Connelly was commander of the Saskatchewan area from 1950 to 1951, and general officer commanding the Prairie Command in 1951; commander, Canadian Military Mission, Far East, 1951 to 1952. He received the Korean Medal, the U.S. Medal and the Coronation Medal. He retired from active service in 1952 with the rank of brigadier, but he remained on the Supplementary List for many years. His rank became brigadier-general when that rank was re-introduced into the Army in the 1960s.

Following is a list of the commanders, Northwest Highway System, through 18 years — 1946 to 1964:

Apr. 1946 to Jan. 1948: Brig. Geoffrey Walsh, CBE, DSO, CD
Jan. 1948 to Sept. 1950: Brig. Allan Burton Connelly, CBE, CD
Dec. 1950 to Apr. 1951: Brig. Ernest C. Brown, CBE, ED, CD
Apr. 1951 to Apr. 1955: Col. Herbert Wainwright Love, OBE, CD
Apr. 1955 to Aug. 1957: Brig. Henry Lloyd Meuser, OBE, CD

Aug. 1957 to Aug. 1960: Brig. J.R.B. Jones, DSO, OBE, CD
Aug. 1960 to Aug. 1962: Brig. L. George C. Lilley, DSO, CD
Aug. 1962 to Aug. 1963: Brig. E.H. Webb, DSO, CD
Aug. 1963 to handover: Brig. G.H. Spencer, OBE, CD

Hope Morritt

Born in Edmonton, Alberta, Hope Morritt attended the University of Western Ontario. She began her writing career as a journalist, and has worked on the *Edmonton Bulletin, Sarnia Observer,* and *London Free Press.* As recounted in this book, Hope also announced and wrote for radio station CFWH, Whitehorse, Yukon.

She is the author of two novels, *Sarah* and *Nahanni,* and a non-fiction work, *Pauline.*

A number of Hope's short stories and articles have appeared in national and international magazines. Three of her plays have been produced on CBC radio. Her poetry has been included in anthologies and in poetry magazines.

Hope Morritt lives in Point Edward, Ontario. She is on the staff of Lambton College in Sarnia, Ontario. A member of the Writers' Union of Canada and the University Women's Club of Canada, Hope is listed in *Contemporary Authors* and *The International Authors and Writers Who's Who.*

Hope and her husband, Dan Cameron, have two children, Lynn and Michael.

191

Index